HEAVENLY
SOLES

HEAVENLY SOLES

Extraordinary Twentieth-Century Shoes

Mary Trasko

Abbeville Press · Publishers · New York · London

Editor: Constance Herndon
Designer : Renée Khatami
Production Editor: Amy Handy
Production Supervisor: Hope Koturo

Half-title page:
*Satin evening mule by Manolo Blahnik.
See Plate 143.*

Title Page:
*Aladdin's Lamp shoe by Herbert Levine, early sixties.
(The Metropolitan Museum of Art, New York. Gift
of Beth and Herbert Levine, New York.) [1]*

Page 5:
*Prototype of Christian Louboutin design in satin,
wood, and leather, 1989. (Christian Louboutin,
Paris.) [2]*

ISBN-13: 978-1-55859-324-4
ISBN-10: 1-55859-324-1

Second edition
10 9 8 7 6 5 4 3

Library of Congress Cataloging-in-Publication Data

Trasko, Mary.
    Heavenly Soles : extraordinary twentieth-century
shoes / Mary Trasko.
    p. cm.
    Bibiography: p.
    Includes index.
    ISBN 1-55859-324-1
    1. Shoes—History—20th century. I. Title.
GT2130.T73 1989
391'.413'0904—dc20   89-6546
                                        CIP

For bulk and premium sales and for text adoption
procedures, write to Customer Service Manager,
Abbeville Press, 137 Varick Street, New York,
NY 10013, or call 1-800-ARTBOOK.

CONTENTS

FOREWORD

Roger Vivier, one of the great designers of our century, has described shoe design as "a sculptural problem in which the center is always a void." Within those simple parameters lies a world of seemingly limitless invention, but one that has remained largely unexplored.

In a book of this length, it is impossible to present the entire history of twentieth-century women's footwear, so I have chosen only the most influential creations, as well as particularly inventive and unusual footwear. The focus here is on high fashion, with relatively little attention to working-class or middle-class shoes, which deserve their own study. On the other hand, quite a few fetish models are depicted, for they were often among the most awe-inspiring shoes of their era, representing footwear's role in a realm beyond a strict fashion context.

The wealth of shoe treasures revealed here comes from some of the world's most enviable collections, public and private. Whenever possible an attempt has been made to acknowledge the individuals and design houses behind these wonderful creations, but unfortunately very little information has been recorded, especially for shoe designers in the early part of the century. While their footwear has played a significant role in underlining the fashion silhouettes of the times, the shoe designers themselves have often gone unrecognized.

See a shoe and Pick it up and all day long you'll have Good Luck

Handcolored lithograph by Andy Warhol, who also did commercial shoe illustrations in the mid-fifties. (George Klauber, New York.)   [3]

ACKNOWLEDGMENTS

A number of people have given me advice, assistance, and encouragement during the creation of this project. First and foremost I would like to thank my editor Constance Herndon, who, knowing of my passion for this subject, invited me to collaborate on what has been a most amusing and pleasurable project. I would also like to extend my most sincere thanks to the photographers, especially Cynthia Hampton and Simon Bocanegra in Paris; David Chambers in London; and Cesar Vera, Cindy Sirko, Jack Carroll, John Hall, Lisa Charles, and Erica Lennard in New York. At Abbeville, Sue Heinemann's copyediting and Renée Khatami's lively design have brought the project to life.

A number of scholars and curators have given me generous advice. I am most grateful to June Swann, curator emeritus of the shoe collection at the Northampton Museum in Northampton, England, whose invaluable insights and critiques have informed much of my research. At the Costume Institute of the Metropolitan Museum of Art in New York, I wish to thank Jean Druesdow, Katell le Bourhis, Margaret van Buskirk, and Kim Fink. I am grateful as well to Stephen de Pietri of the Yves Saint Laurent Archive, Paris; Denise Dixon-Smith of the Central Museum, Northampton, England; and Jonathan Walford of the Bata Shoe Museum Foundation in Toronto. Marie-Josephe Bossan of the Musée de la

Chaussure in Romans, France, and Pierre Provoyeur of the Musée des Arts de la Mode in Paris kindly provided permission to reproduce photographs, as did Salvatore Ferragamo, SpA, Bally of Switzerland, the Yves Saint Laurent Archive, Charles Jourdan, Sonja Bata, Eleanor Lambert, Joseph Vasta, Gérard Benoit-Vivier, and the Fondation Cartier, Paris.

Individuals who lent shoes for photography included Diana Vreeland, Katell le Bourhis, Susanne Bartsch, John Badum, and Beth and Herbert Levine in New York; Roger Vivier, Gaetana Coda (née Di Mauro), and Billyboy in Paris. For their generosity I am most grateful.

Finally, my personal thanks to Mr. and Mrs. Leo Trasko and Len Trasko, Jane and John Stubbs, Franck Giraud, and Stephen Szczepanek. And a big thanks to Joanne Cassullo and Jeffrey Kalinsky of Barneys New York.

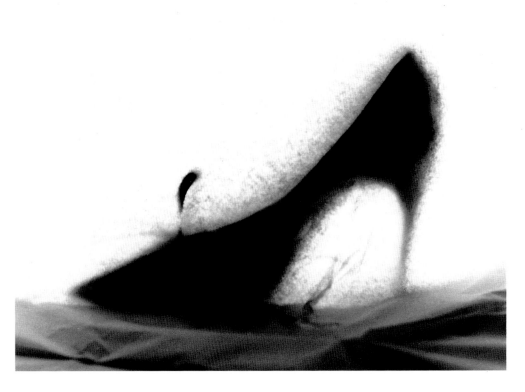

Stiletto pump from the fifties by Roger VIVIER. (Private collection.) [4]

9

INTRODUCTION

Fabled ruby slippers worn by Judy Garland in The Wizard of Oz, *designed by Hollywood costume designer Gilbert ADRIAN, 1938. His first Arabian-style test pair was deemed too exotic for Dorothy. (Private collection.)* [5]

How lovely are thy feet with shoes, oh prince's daughter.
—Song of Solomon 4:1

Women, and a great many men, have long been captivated by the special magic of shoes. As our contact with the earth, they may be practical necessities, but they can also be more seductively sculptural than any other element of fashion, inspiring enough caprice and imaginative longing to set the mind reeling.

Probably the most fabled of all shoes were the ruby slippers worn by Judy Garland in *The Wizard of Oz.* Following the legendary Hollywood costume designer Adrian's model, not one but eight pairs were made, the smaller sizes used for closeup shots. When one of the pairs came up for auction at Christie's in New York in June 1988, it sold for $165,000, making it the most expensive pair of shoes ever purchased. Asked what he intended to do with his ruby slippers, the anonymous buyer replied ecstatically, "Treasure them."

For centuries women's feet and their coverings have held an oddly exalted position. In the late sixteenth century Italian potters made hand warmers in the shape of women's shoes, which noblemen cupped in their hands both for warmth and "to enjoy pleasant recollections."[1] In more recent times the duke of Windsor had a passionate foot fetish, which the duchess gleefully indulged.[2] The duke may be among the most renowned, but psychologists maintain that a fascination with feet and shoes is the most common form of sexual fetishism in Western society. Goethe, the great German poet, dramatist, and novelist, once wrote to Christiane

Vulpuis, his wife, "... send me your latest new shoes you told me about, with their soles danced through, just to give me something belonging to you again, to press against my heart."[3]

Until the twentieth century women's feet were considered a symbol of chastity, a private part to be hidden from view. As late as 1840 a gentleman in Paris observed, "Look a Parisienne in the eye and her face registers not a trace of emotion, but gaze at her feet and she blushes and turns away."[4] So strong was the sexual symbolism of the foot that in seventeenth-century Spain when Queen Maria Luisa of Savoy, the wife of Philip V, fell off her horse and was dragged around the palace courtyard with her foot caught in the stirrup, several lords just looked on in horror—to help her would mean touching her foot, a fiercely taboo act. The man who finally saved her had to take refuge in a monastery until he received a royal pardon for his act.[5]

Over the centuries shoes have also expressed social power, symbolizing men's authority over women and effectively enslaving women by circumscribing their mobility. The symbolism can clearly be seen in some of the rituals of the marriage ceremony. In the Middle Ages, for example, a father's authority over his daughter was passed to her husband by means of her shoe. In other instances the groom might hand the bride a shoe; to put it on was to concede that she had become his subject.

Perhaps the most potent example of the use of footwear to enhance men's authority (and thereby their pleasure?) is the Chinese custom of foot-binding, which began in the tenth century and continued until 1911 when the Chinese republic was founded. Girls aged four to six, sometimes younger, were subjected to this excruciatingly painful ritual, which ultimately shaped their identity. Women with unbound feet often served as second wives or slaves to these favored women who, after enduring the deformations, could only mince along with painful, delicate steps—a gait that men found deliriously erotic.

The bound feet themselves, called lily feet, were treated as an extremely private domain, to be viewed only by a woman's husband and otherwise kept covered at all times. A French doctor traveling in China in 1899 noted that the unshod, deformed foot was thought to be exquisitely beautiful; touching it brought on feelings "similar to the European sensibility in touching a woman's breast...purely a question of sentiment and of sensation."[6]

In the Western world small feet were

Chinese nineteenth-century embroidered lotus shoe with plaster cast of lotus foot. (Musée de la Chaussure, Romans.) [6]

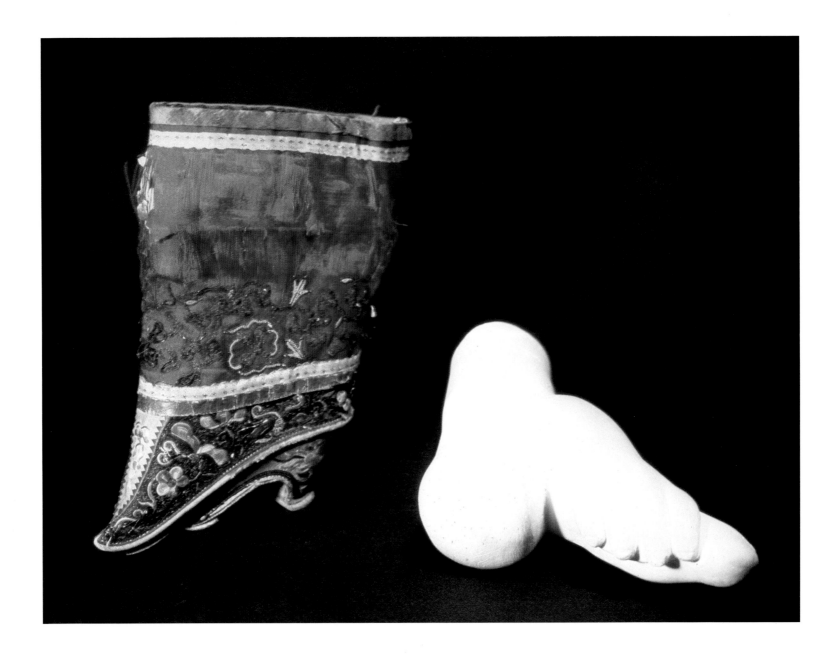

also regarded as aristocratic, a most exquisite expression of femininity. Even though the practice of wearing shoes of the smallest possible size caused the bones of the feet to become twisted and deformed, it appeared and reappeared from the Renaissance to the Victorian era. Just as the corset created the illusion of a tiny waist, so might a tightly buttoned boot pinch in the foot, leaving a bulge of flesh above, as engravings of the period sometimes show. Once anesthetics were introduced in the 1860s, some women even had one or two toes removed to better endure wearing the extremely narrow shoes of the period.[7]

Bizarre examples abound of the ways that shoes were used to control women's mobility. Indeed, immobility was indicative of an aristocratic standard—the less a woman walked, the higher her social prominence. From medieval times, women of the *beau monde* in England, France, Italy, and Spain moved about in some form of sedan chair or litter, in most cases being carried directly into the room. In sixteenth-century Venice, extremely high platforms became fashionable—so high that ladies required the support of an escort or maid in order to walk. (The highest platforms in a Venetian collection are two feet, three inches tall,

although the models higher than nine inches show little evidence of wear.) The Venetian women, who traveled primarily by gondola, apparently adopted the style from Turkish harem women, who walked even less. Interestingly, some noblemen disapproved of the fashion, which allowed the ladies to tower over them, but the church sanctioned it because it was thought that if women couldn't move around freely, dancing and so on, there would be fewer possibilities for sin. Insubstantial footwear had a similarly restrictive effect on women's movement. In the 1830s, for example, women's shoes were so flimsy that their wearers could not stray far from home.

In the twentieth century shoes have continued to embody certain attitudes toward women's power and place in society. Although women today enjoy much greater freedom of movement, with footwear perfected for fit, comfort, and balance, it has not been a steady evolution toward comfort (witness the stiletto heel), nor is the liberation total. Recent studies indicate that as many as forty-five percent of American women sometimes wear shoes that hurt in order to look fashionable,[8] and one leading scholar has estimated that the percentage for European women, who tend not to walk as much as their American counterparts, is considerably higher.[9] Yet women now have a significant choice: they can walk home in Reeboks and later slip on a pair of stiletto heels for a night on the town. Women today are perhaps more aware of the sexual politics inherent in shoe design, but the allure of shoes continues to thrive.

CHAPTER ONE

Setting the Stage for the Grand Luxe of Paris

*Left, high-button custom-made boots,
c. 1900, for the Duchesse de Galea. Above,
embroidered French satin boot by the design house
of PINET, 1875. (Above, Musée de la Mode
et du Costume, Paris; left, Musée de la
Chaussure, Romans.) [8–9]*

*The Duke cried in a terrifying voice:
"Oriane, what have you been thinking
of, you wretch! You've kept on your
black shoes! With a red dress! Go
upstairs quick and put on red shoes…"*
—Marcel Proust,
Remembrance of Things Past[1]

Proust recreated this dialogue from
a scene he once witnessed, when his
friend Madame Strauss attempted the
above combination, much to the dismay
of her husband—an indication of how
seriously Parisians took the elaborate
system of signals that made up the
reigning fashion culture. That highly so-
phisticated culture, coupled with the su-
periority of the local clothing industries,
has made Paris the world capital of
fashion for more than three centuries.
At least as early as 1815, and throughout the nineteenth century, France

flooded England and the United States
with Parisian footwear, which was in
turn widely copied. The exuberant patronage provided by the Parisian gentry
into the late nineteenth century allowed
such fine custom footwear houses as
Pinet to flourish, although in many other
shoemaking centers things had begun
to change.

The second half of the nineteenth
century, characterized by the social and
economic reorganization of so many aspects of daily life, brought great
changes in the manufacture of shoes.
The replacement of hand tools with machinery and the introduction of factory
production revolutionized the shoemaker's métier. Although shoemaking in
previous eras had offered little financial
reward, it had at least provided a high
degree of job satisfaction. For centuries
the making of shoes had involved a
lively social interaction between the

shoemaker and the client; even people of modest means had consulted a shoemaker for their footwear, just as it was not unusual for a tailor to have made their clothes. Now all that began to change.

As early as the seventeenth century, England had developed a system of mass production to fabricate great quantities of army boots that involved a division of manual labor. In the late eighteenth century mass production was in place in shoemaking towns such as Northampton, although shoe parts were still handcrafted. By the 1850s, however, the mechanization of the footwear industry began in earnest, first with the sewing machine and soon after with the riveting machine. Alarm spread among shoemakers, who feared unemployment and lower wages as the uses of machinery spread and as women entered the labor market. Boycotts and protests were launched, but they were ultimately short-lived. By the time the twentieth century opened, traditional cobblers were being replaced by a factory assembly system in which all or selected parts of the shoe were machine-made. The place and function of the shoemaker had been taken over by the "cutter," "clicker," "riveter," and "machine girl."[2] Shoemaking was no longer a highly es-

teemed craft; indeed the great shoe designer Salvatore Ferragamo, who came from a poor family in Italy, noted their sharp disappointment when, around 1905, he informed them of his desired vocation.

The second half of the nineteenth century also brought changes in the construction of shoes. Until this time the majority of shoes in the Western world were not differentiated left from right. (In the East many traditional shoe styles continue to be made identically.) When the first left- and right-footed

Prize-winning boot in black patent and morocco leather with forty-four stitches to the inch, by J. HEWLETT of Northampton, 1873. (Northampton Museums and Art Gallery, Northampton, England.) [10]

Gilt glacé kidskin shoe by Charles HIND of London, c. 1890, with five-inch wooden heels covered by engraved and gilded plaster; a metal heel plate at the bottom protects the fragile plaster-work, which has been slightly chipped. (Northampton Museums and Art Gallery, Northampton, England.)   [11]

shoes were made in Philadelphia some-time between 1801 and 1822, they were viewed as crooked. Some of the resistance was due to a certain modesty on the part of women, who did not wish to show the shape of their feet in such a pronounced fashion. After the 1860s, however, most quality shoes were distin-guished left from right, and by the 1880s "straights" had all but disap-peared. In that decade the current system of full and half sizes was estab-lished in the United States and Britain.

Inevitably shoe fashions also under-went changes in the Victorian era. Boots and shoes became almost unisex, with any ostentatious decoration viewed as an inducement to immorality. Out-doors, women typically wore boots with high tops and eight to twenty buttons— a style that remained popular as a fash-ion boot until the mid-twenties. Slippers and pumps, on the other hand, were restricted to inside wear.

Even though the aniline dyes invented around 1865 made vivid colors possible, such as bright green, purple, and fuch-sia, most of the shoes produced before and during the First World War came in a limited color range. Walking shoes were black, gray, tan, or white, while evening shoes were generally bronze or black. Heels were also conservative, typically two to two and a half inches high in a style known as the Louis heel. In the 1890s, however, heels as high as six and a half inches swept into fashion and remained in vogue until the turn of the century. Yet dresses were still long enough to conceal footwear during these years.

The last decades of the nineteenth century were filled with dramatic if con-flicting developments in the realm of costume. A number of fashion trends suggested a new freedom and a gradual

Two Viennese fetish shoes from around 1900—
that on the left inspired by boudoir slippers, in
black kidskin and blue satin with enameled buttons and eight-inch heels, and on the right, one in
Bordeaux-colored kidskin with an eleven-inch
heel covered in black leather. (Musée de la
Chaussure, Romans.)   [12–13]

Below, an anonymous shoemaker's display,
probably English, c. 1900–10, showing a variety of high heels and several models in patent
leather, a finish developed around 1800 after experimentation with different enamels.   [14]

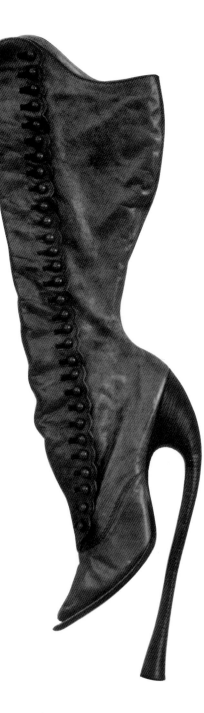

Beaded evening slippers by HELLSTERN AND SONS, c. 1900, for Comtesse Elisabeth Greffuhle, the beautiful sovereign of Parisian Belle Epoque society. (Musée de la Mode et du Costume, Paris.) [15]

increase in mobility for women. The 1890s brought clothing and shoes designed for the newly active woman, whose sporting activities included tennis, yachting, and bicycling. But these fashions were strictly regulated. In Paris, for example, a woman could wear bloomers in public to bicycle in the park, but she was forbidden to appear on the street in trousers without the company of her bicycle.

During the *belle époque* in Paris, however, upper-class women's fashion continued to be a sumptuous, high-maintenance affair. At fashionable country outings and picnics, women appeared in the same finery they wore in town, and, as one historian of fashion explains, there was a reason: "Long skirts, fragile hats, narrow shoes with high heels—all that could impede walking and make women seem helpless filled their husbands with self-importance. With the wives unable to put one foot in front of the other unaided, the open-air craze could not but enhance the authority of men."[3]

Paris was unique in its emphasis on "seeing and being seen" and in the importance placed on clothing as a signifier of cultural prominence. Shoe design, like other aspects of fashion, benefited from the marvelous alchemy of masterful craftsmanship and generous patronage. Indeed, the superb styling of Parisian footwear came to be copied throughout the world. While traditional shoemaking towns were coming to terms with mechanization, custom-crafted footwear was thriving in Paris.

Parisian women chose their shoes with care. The custom-made boots of heiress Anna Gould, in a simple lace-up style in reptile and leather, splendidly finished, were typical of what wealthy women wore around 1900. The Duchesse de Galea had her boots subtly distinguished by fine decorative stitching and an undulating top. More colorful and brazenly decorated were the boots of La Belle Otéro, one of the leading courtesans of the day, who was known to "jump up onto a table at Maxim's and go into a writhing fandango so sensual that every man in the room felt she was making love to him."[4]

Women in New York at the turn of the century, on the other hand, were interested in different issues. They were walking more, so shoe widths took on new importance; Cammeyer, a store in New York, offered five widths in 1904. A masculine style of evening pump was widely adopted as a street and carriage shoe, as was the oxford, a low-cut laced style originally designed to serve as a

kind of corset for the foot to keep it from spreading. Suffragettes signaled their emancipation by wearing sturdy leather shoes with flat, sensible heels. Shedding any pretensions to tiny feet, they rejected the narrow-lasted models that for so long had crippled women. Comfort became a consideration, one that gained even greater importance in the teens as women joined the war effort.

When men went off to war, women were called into the labor force to build up armaments; by 1915 in France, for example, women made up one quarter

of all workers in munitions factories, and shoe styles reflected their increased presence in a number of professions. High-cut lace-up boots with relatively low heels, up to only two inches high—a suitable style for active women—were typical during the war. Since there were no material shortages as there would be during World War II, the majority of these day shoes were made in leather. Evening shoes, however, were a different matter, often styled in sumptuous fabrics and influenced by the decorative trends taking hold in Paris.

The war did not put an end to high fashion by any means. As the fighting approached Paris, legions of wealthy but dispossessed men and women descended on Deauville, where Gabrielle (Coco) Chanel was experiencing her first success as an *haute couturière*. She offered long, loosely fitted ensembles of the simplicity and slim line that were to become the hallmarks of her style. Her concept was revolutionary, considering that most women's fashion until then had accentuated the fullness of the female figure—sometimes, as with the bustle, to the point of caricature. Other designers, too, began to offer simply styled clothes in reaction to the highly structured, elaborate clothes then in vogue. Chanel sensed that finally, in 1914, the

Haute monde *and* demimonde: *custom-made boots, c. 1900—on the left, a lace-up style for the American heiress Anna Gould, and, at right, a pair with elaborately inlaid leather for La Belle Otéro, a leading courtesan. (Left, Musée de la Mode et du Costume, Paris; right, Musée de la Chaussure, Romans.)* [16–17]

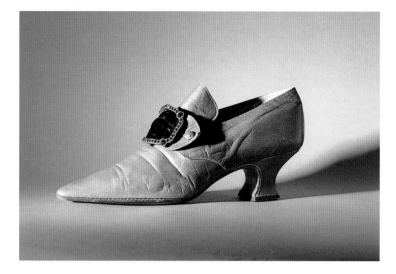

modern era was arriving: "A world was dying while another was being born.... I was in attendance at the death of luxury, at the demise of the nineteenth century, and also at the end of an era."[5]

But luxury did not disappear entirely. During the war years in Paris, a designer named Pietro Yantourny continued to create custom-made shoes of an exquisite refinement. These shoes, with their long, narrow shapes and splendid toes, exhibited a level of craftsmanship that seemed to belong to another century. Although Yantourny worked with established forms, such as the spectator or the buckled evening pump, his artistry was such that the silhouettes became completely his own. At the top under the buckle, for instance,

he might add a high, deftly curved tongue—a flourish that emphasized the graceful curve at the top of a woman's foot.

Yantourny worked from an upperfloor salon just off the Place Vendôme, one of the most chic shopping areas in Paris. At street level a placard announced: *Le bottier le plus cher du monde* ("The world's most expensive custom shoemaker"). His was an exclusive trade, offering shoes for sport, hunting, evening, and town, shown by appointment only. Yantourny sold mostly to wealthy English and American women, among them Nancy Lancaster and Millicent Rogers.

Undoubtedly his best patron was Rita de Acosta Lydig, who commis-

Leather pump by *HELLSTERN AND SONS, c. 1900, accented with black velvet and a green rhinestone buckle. (The Metropolitan Museum of Art, New York. Gift of Mrs. Edward A. Morrison.)* [18]

Pink satin pumps by *HELLSTERN AND SONS, 1910, with original box. (Bata Shoe Museum Foundation, Toronto.)* [19]

Evening pump by Pietro YANTOURNY, c. 1911–15, with rhinestone buckle, V-shaped tongue, and two-inch Louis heels. (The Metropolitan Museum of Art, New York. Gift of Howard Sturges.) [20]

sioned more than three hundred pairs of shoes, even though she never walked more than short distances. Described as "one of the most elegant women of all time" by Diana Vreeland,[6] Lydig was not concerned only with fashion—she was also a generous patron of the arts as well as an advocate of women's suffrage and birth control. Still, as Cecil Beaton notes, "Mrs. Lydig graced the opening cycles of the twentieth century with a perfectionism that would have been rare in any period since the Renaissance."[7] During the day she might wear spectators or buckle shoes, while in the evening she could choose from magnificent shoes Yantourny had embroidered with lace and velvets she herself provided. (She was an avid collector of antique textiles.) All the shoes were extremely lightweight.

Although Yantourny created some of

Trunk full of YANTOURNY evening shoes, c. 1915, embroidered with antique textiles for Rita de Acosta Lydig. The trunk, in Russian leather lined with velvet, was accompanied by a similar case for day shoes. (The Metropolitan Museum of Art, New York. Gift of Capezio, Inc.) [21]

Lace-embroidered shoe by YANTOURNY from Lydig's evening trunk. (The Metropolitan Museum of Art, New York. Gift of Capezio, Inc.) [22]

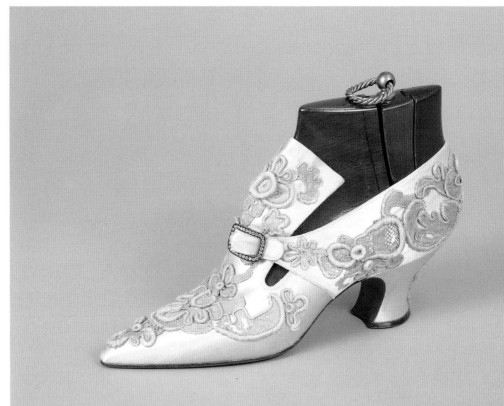

Spectator by YANTOURNY, c. 1915, from Lydig's day trunk. (The Metropolitan Museum of Art, New York. Gift of Capezio, Inc.) [23]

the most exquisite shoes of this century, very little has been written about his life or his work. A short but illuminating portrait is provided in the autobiography of Mercedes de Acosta, who frequently accompanied her sister for her shoe fittings. She describes Yantourny as East Indian by birth, a vegetarian, and an extremely ascetic person. (There are conflicting reports of his nationality; judging from his name, he may have been at least partly Italian.) Having once served as the curator of the shoe collection at the Cluny Museum,

"There was nothing he didn't know about shoes of every period," Mercedes remarks. "He went into designing shoes because he had a passion for them."[8]

Yantourny was selective about his clientele, she remembers. A deposit of $1,000 was required to begin work, and he was in no hurry to complete orders: "You could count on the first pair being delivered in about two years. If he liked you very much, as he did Rita, you might hope to get them in a year, or if a miracle occurred, six months." Ordering shoes from Yantourny might require great patience and a deep purse, but the results were well worth the wait. These were shoes of incomparable elegance, which fit, in Beaton's words, "like a silk sock."[9] In addition to measuring every inch of the foot and making a plaster cast, he would observe his client walking barefoot so he could see where the weight was placed. He confessed to Mercedes that he loved making shoes for her sister Rita because "she...is the only person I know who, as she walks, places her feet correctly on the ground."[10]

With Yantourny and Chanel defining its contrasts, the period of shoe design from 1885 to 1920 was one of dramatic transition, one in which "the delicacy of Edwardian design was challenged by Art Nouveau, Cubism and other art movements."[11] In Paris by the late teens, simple lines and forms, luxurious in execution, began to prevail in fashion, textiles, and the decorative arts— culminating in the Art Deco style of the International Arts Exposition of 1925. Hemlines went up, exposing legs and feet and creating a new interest in shoes. Buttons and laces began to disappear in favor of simple shapes covered with fine fabrics and intricate leatherwork.

It was in 1920 that André Perugia

established himself in Paris. In a career spanning more than fifty years, this designer would present some of the most startlingly inventive heels and silhouettes ever created. Born in the late 1890s into a family of Italian shoemakers living in Nice, Perugia worked in his father's shop from age eleven. In his late teens he began showing his own models in the hall of one of the major hotels along the city's promenade. One of his first customers was a kept woman—extremely well kept—who was dressed by the couturier Paul Poiret. Thanks to her Poiret noticed Perugia's shoes and, during a trip to Nice in 1914, asked him to show them in Poiret's house in Paris. But the war intervened and Perugia went to work at a factory constructing airplanes, an activity that influenced his later work considerably. As he explained, "A pair of shoes must be perfect like an equation, and adjusted to the millimeter like a motor piece."[12]

After the war Perugia went to Paris at last and began making shoes for Poiret, receiving a marvelous introduction into the world of Paris fashion. In general Perugia's shoes from the twenties followed the most popular styles— T-straps and bar shoes (the latter a shoe with a single strap across the front

Evening shoes by André PERUGIA, early 1920s, with metallic finish and oriental motifs, probably created to accompany an ensemble by Paul Poiret. (Billyboy, Paris.) [24]

fastened with a button). He also made divinely shaped pumps and backless shoes, and often his designs were decorated with geometric patterns, skillfully laid in leather. One inventive design from the late twenties, topped with dice and sporting heels resembling dominoes, suggested his beginnings in Nice, where the casinos were a popular pastime.

houses the center of world fashion.

Clothing designs of the period emphasized sports and freedom of movement, with Jean Patou, Coco Chanel, and, a few years later, Elsa Schiaparelli offering simple models easily adapted to mass production—the beginnings of ready-to-wear. Chanel was particularly influential, popularizing classic dressing

itty leather model with domino heels by PERUGIA, 1929, for strolling to the casino in style. (Musée Charles Jourdan, Romans.) [25]

The twenties in Paris were a time of extravagance and high living. As Toto Kooperman, then a mannequin for Chanel, observed, this was a time when women really dressed up—in lace, jewels, and hats—"not to please men, but to astound other women."[13] In 1924 the French franc was devalued 280 percent and foreigners flocked to Paris on a spending spree, making the couture

for comfort, including separates, sweaters and tweeds, and cardigan suits.

Fashionable women shopped in Paris not only for clothing but also for such fine accessories as printed-silk shoes or fishnet stockings tied by hand. Although the bar shoe fastened with a single button was the predominant style of the time, women could choose from a seemingly unlimited variety of fabrics or

vening shoes with bas-relief embroidery in gold thread, and beveled, embossed metal heels—extravagant models custom-made for Mistinguett, the legendary star of the Parisian music hall revues whose legs were insured for a million dollars. The matching bag was a fashion that began in the 1920s. (Musée de la Mode et du Costume, Paris.) [26]

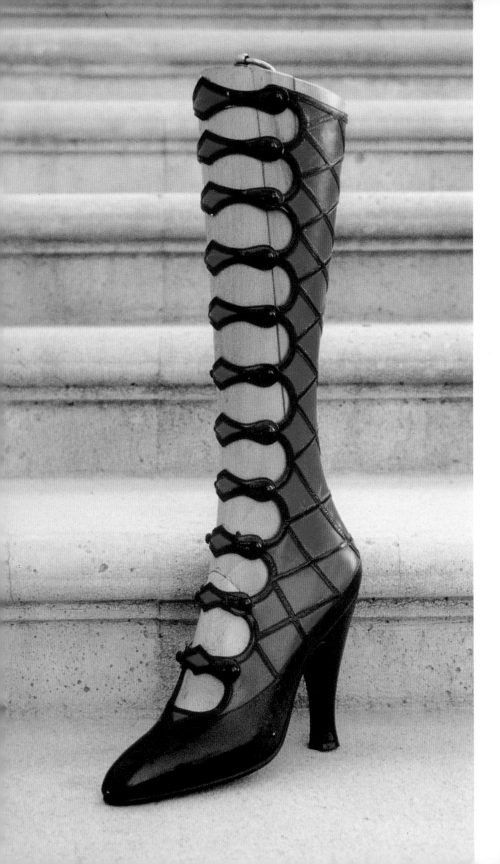

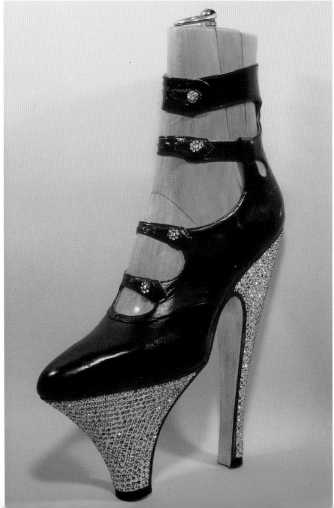

leather, and heels decorated with rhinestones, enamelwork, cloisonné, or embossed metal. Lizard and crocodile were also widely available for women's shoes by the mid-1920s. And a greatly expanded palette of colors, including many bright shades for daytime wear, signaled the gay, increasingly hopeful mood after the war. Even buckles took on a new character and became very jewel-like, in line with the passion for costume jewelry created by Chanel.

As all this suggests, the demand for luxury shoes continued to thrive, met by houses like Hellstern and Argence. Established in Paris by Louis Hellstern around 1870, Hellstern reached a peak of production and its creative zenith from 1920 to 1925 under the direction of the three Hellstern sons, Maurice, Charles, and Henri. Charles was responsible between 1920 and 1930 for styling women's shoes, which consisted primarily of bar shoes, very stylish boots, and pumps with Louis heels of two to three inches. Although the shape was standard, these shoes came in a wide variety of materials including suede, kidskin, and various reptiles dyed in brilliant shades of violet, green, fuchsia, yellow, and red. Rhinestone buttons played an important decorative role, as did shoe buckles of painted

metal and pearls, some inlaid with marcasite. Lavish boots for day and evening were a specialty of the house, which also created some of the most extravagant fetish boots ever made with heels up to ten and a half inches high. (The fetish models included high, rhinestoned platforms, a precursor to the styles so fashionable in the late 1930s.) Among the clientele were many European princes and princesses, stage actresses, and wealthy Parisians, some of whom bought three pairs per week (paying for their shoes monthly, quarterly, or yearly, and spending a veritable fortune).

Another house of luxury shoes specializing in decorated heels and buckles in the 1920s was Argence, founded in 1900. Their rhinestone heels were widely copied in the twenties and early thirties by other French houses and by shoe manufacturers in New York. The principal designer in the 1920s was Alfred Victoria Argence, who made shoes for the royal families of England, Belgium, Spain, Italy, and Romania, as well as members of the Vanderbilt, Carnegie, Taft, and Morgan families in the United States.

The unparalleled craftsmanship and invention exhibited in Paris had a far-reaching influence throughout America and Europe. But it was also at this

*S*ilver leather shoe with rhinestone buckle from the late 1920s; below, buckle and decorated heel c. 1925—all by Alfred Victoria ARGENCE. (Musée de la Chaussure, Romans.) [30–32]

Sporty, late 1920s day shoe in white chamois leather by BALLY of Switzerland, a design house established in the early 1800s that was one of the few outside of Paris able to rival French craftsmanship. (Bally Museum, Schoenenwerd, Switzerland.) [33]

time, around 1920, that a new designer was becoming established in California, one who also emphasized handcrafting in an increasingly mechanized industry and who made comfort a hallmark of his stylish designs. His name was Salvatore Ferragamo.

From an early age, Ferragamo had apprenticed with shoemakers in his native Bonito in Italy as well as in Naples, and by the time he was fourteen he ran a studio of six craftsmen in Bonito, all older than himself. In 1914 he came to America to help his brothers with their shop in Santa Barbara, the love of craftsmanship deeply instilled in him.

His brothers were impressed by the vast quantities of shoes that American companies could produce by machine, but Salvatore found the machine-made shoes to be "heavy, clumsy, graceless, with points like potatoes and heels like lead."[14] The reduced cost did not, in his opinion, justify such an inferior product.

Ferragamo was appalled by the sorry condition of nearly all the feet he saw and by the pads and cushions people used to line their shoes just to make them wearable, and so he devoted himself to the problem of creating a comfortable, wearable shoe. At the local

university, he studied anatomy, particularly the skeletal structure of the foot. After learning that the entire weight of the body dropped straight onto the arches of the feet, he inserted a thin steel plate in the arch of the shoe for better support. With his custom-made shoes, he began experimenting with a system of thirteen measurements for an exacting fit that left room for the toes and the heel to flex freely.

Among the Ferragamo brothers' early clients was the American Film Company, which ordered large quantities of shoes for the costume and historical dramas of D.W. Griffith and Cecil B. DeMille. One of Ferragamo's boots for these spectacles was so comfortable that DeMille exclaimed, "The West would have been conquered earlier, if they had had boots like these!"[15]

By 1923 Ferragamo moved the shop

to Hollywood, where orders for his shoes greatly increased, thanks to the patronage of Mary Pickford, Rudolph Valentino, Douglas Fairbanks, Pola Negri, and Clara Bow. Inspired by cubist and futurist art, his designs were boldly geometric with a sleek silhouette. Quite often the heels were at least three inches high, but always with rounded toes and room for the foot to flex. After personally taking the client's foot measurements, he would experiment with a new pattern directly on the wooden form, without working from sketches.

Unable to find the craftsmen in Hollywood to fill his orders, Ferragamo moved back to Italy in 1927. In the next decade he devised a revolutionary method of hand production, a kind of human assembly line reminiscent of the mass production methods of earlier centuries under which each worker had learned a specialized part of the shoe-making process. He offered young, unemployed men (and, as photographs show, a few women) the chance to learn a trade while earning a small salary.

Based in Florence, he exported a great many shoes to stores in New York, California, Chicago, as well as England, establishing early on a special cachet for the "Made in Italy" label.

CHAPTER TWO

Enter the Clodhopper

Everywhere in the streets, there were dazzling girls, cycling, crawling up tank turrets.... They were top-heavy with built-up pompadour-front hair-dos and waving tresses; weighted to the ground with clumsy, fancy thick-soled wedge shoes.
—Lee Miller, reporting for *Vogue* from wartime Paris[1]

After the Depression, high-fashion shoes were brightly colored, but in the thirties most women's shoes came in dismal, muddy colors, perhaps reflecting the prevailing mood. People had a sense of foreboding, of another war coming on. "You felt it in everything," Diana Vreeland remembers. "Everything was weakening."[2] At the same time films about high society, a popular escape from the Depression doldrums, were transmitting fashion ideas more quickly than ever before, including the importance of well-shod feet to the ensemble. T-straps and bar shoes remained popular until the mid-thirties, with heels generally three inches or a bit higher. A growing league of manufacturers who specialized in comfort shoes, however, issued warnings on the dangers of high heels. One Milwaukee shoe company charged that wearing heels that were too high could cause "headaches, insomnia, dizziness, eye trouble, nervousness and constipation."[3] While these claims were exaggerated, women were indeed discovering that wearing high heels continuously caused the calf muscles to atrophy and made it painful to wear shoes of a different heel height.

For a while sandals came into fashion. Although Madeleine Vionnet had shown sandals with her simply cut dresses in 1907, they were considered

"*Les Quatres Grands*" liberation shoe by Camille DI MAURO, 1944, with Allied flag details in suede and kidskin. (Di Mauro, Paris.) [35]

Change in silhouette shown in models from MR. BOB, Inc. of New York: above, group of evening models, c. 1927–29, and right, striped fabric pump, mid-1930s. (The Metropolitan Museum of Art, New York. Above, beige satin gift of Mrs. R.C. Jacobsen. Other three gift of Mrs. Lee Ault and Mrs. Ray Hill in memory of Mrs. Charles R. Leonard. Striped model gift of Julia B. Henry.)   [36–37]

Two anonymous fetish photographs, c. 1937–39, suggesting that rounder toes even affected the styling of fetish footwear. [38–39]

odd and were not adopted for general wear.[4] Before the thirties nudity of the foot was considered unchaste, but by the start of the decade clear vinyl sandals with rhinestone-studded plastic heels were shown in New York by Seymour Troy and Edouard, two of the city's most successful creators of custom-made and fine footwear. Open styles then became less available during wartime, when there were strict guidelines for shoe design, but afterward they were again in fashion.

In general, by 1935 shoe styles were moving toward chunkier heels and rounder toes, a sturdier look that would prevail during the war years. Lady Mendl (Elsie de Wolfe), a great influence in fashion and decorating, was frequently photographed wearing round-toed shoes for added comfort. In March 1935 Paris *Vogue* showed Chanel's evening gowns with flat-heeled, black satin shoes, an idea readopted by many designers in the 1980s.

The aftermath of the Depression

brought lean times for the Parisian couture houses. Thousands in the industry were out of work because of customs barriers, and nationalistic slogans advised to "Buy American" or "Buy British." Only the savviest thrived: Chanel, for example, with her understated smartness, or Schiaparelli with her witty and conversation-making designs. The rivalry between the two heated up as they both courted a small coterie of glamorous American women—among them Millicent Rogers, Diana Vreeland, and Mona Williams (Mrs. Harrison Williams). As the *New York Times* reported, by 1935 such women made up half of the "Best-Dressed List," a poll started by the Parisian fashion designers in the previous decade. In addition to exhibiting poise and vivacity, the *Times* had reported, a candidate for the Best-Dressed List had to spend at least $50,000 in the Parisian dressmaking trade—although some stylish Americans were given a reduced price, or not charged at all, because they brought designers so much publicity.[5]

Paris continued to be an influential center of shoe design in the thirties. Perugia, who had moved to 4 rue de la Paix, began designing shoes for Schiaparelli, who was in the same building.

Their association continued for at least a decade, with Perugia making footwear to accompany her designs under his ready-to-wear label "Padova," as well as special-order boots for Schiap

herself in leopard and monkey fur. Among his innovations for Schiaparelli were stretch shoes made from strips of crosshatched suede with elastic fittings that eliminated the need for buckles or buttons.

Model by PERUGIA worn by Josephine Baker in the film Zou Zou, *1934. (Musée Charles Jourdan, Romans.)* [40]

Pair of suede and monkey-fur boots custom-made for Elsa Schiaparelli by PERUGIA, 1938. (Philadelphia Museum of Art. Given by Madame Elsa Schiaparelli.) [41]

In 1933 Camille Di Mauro established his design house at 14 rue Faubourg Saint Honoré, offering fine made-to-order shoes. Di Mauro had learned the trade at age seven in his native Sicily and had later, in the mid-twenties, worked with Perugia. He was a master craftsman, finishing his models with fine marquetry in leather and fabric and decorative stitching. His shoes repre-

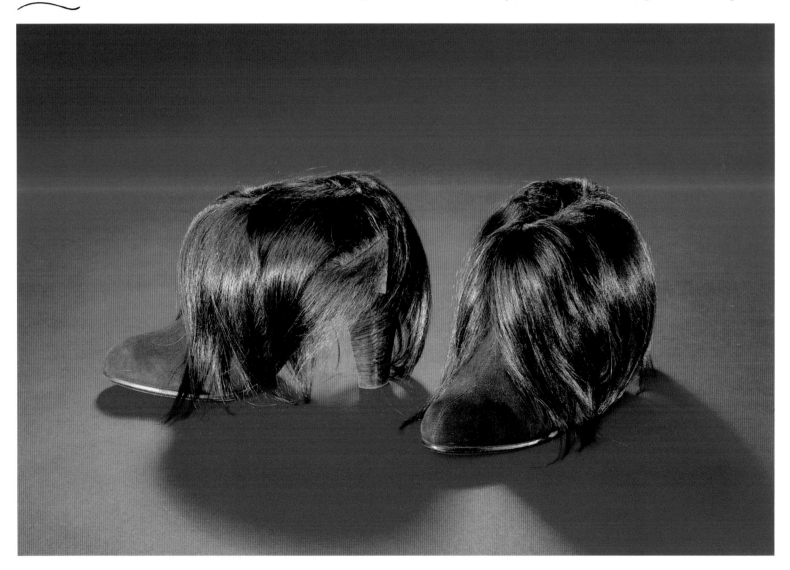

*S*ketches by SCHIAPARELLI for the Shoe Hat, 1937. Pen on paper. (Musée des Arts de la Mode, Paris. Collection of Union des Arts Décoratifs.)   [43]

*B*lack suede lace-up shoe by PERUGIA for Schiaparelli, 1937—the model for Schiaparelli's Shoe Hat of the same year. (Billyboy, Paris.)   [42]

Counterclockwise from left: group of heels by Camille DI MAURO from 1931, exhibiting masterful marquetry in leather and fabrics; DI MAURO in the 1920s with his young son, Yanno; "In Memory of Yanno," 1935, suede shoe commemorating the untimely death of his son. The shoe could be ordered with a picture of the client's choice for the cameo. (Di Mauro, Paris.) [44–46]

sented the splendid craftsmanship available in Paris during the thirties and forties in spite of the wartime restrictions.

It was also in the mid-thirties that Georgette became one of the first women to design under her own label. Although there were many renowned women fashion designers in Paris, such as the Callot Sisters, Madeleine Vionnet, Jeanne Lanvin, Madame Alix Grès, Chanel, and Schiaparelli, little is known about women shoe designers, most of whom probably worked for large design houses and thus were not credited for their creations. Even with Georgette, the information is limited; her family name, for example, is never mentioned. What is known is that she worked as the principal saleswoman at Perugia, where her brother Etienne was the *formiste*, handcrafting the shoes and ensuring women a proper fit. The brother-sister team opened their own shop at 22 rue Cambon in the mid-thirties and enjoyed the patronage of many fashionable women of the period.[6] Their styling was simple, classic, and elegant, executed with a remarkably skilled hand.

During the same period Roger Vivier began designing shoes out of a workshop on the Place Vendôme, where upper-floor studios were cheap and plentiful. Vivier had studied sculpture at the Ecole des Beaux-Arts, but an apprenticeship at a shoe factory employing both machine and hand production gave his sculptural interests a new direction. At first he designed shoe samples for a German leather company that supplied many of the large European shoe companies. Several clients admired his samples and in no time Vivier was designing models for Pinet and Bally in France, Salamander and Mercedes in Germany, Rayne and Turner in England, and Delman in the United States. In 1937 Vivier opened his own design house at 22 rue Royale and was soon designing exclusively for Delman, one of the most respected American manufacturers of fine-quality shoes, who, by the thirties, retailed through Bergdorf Goodman in New York City.

In Italy, Ferragamo was recovering from financial difficulties brought on by the devalued dollar and by problems in implementing the production system for his handmade shoes. Although forced to cease production in 1933, he was back in business the following year and by 1936 had acquired the thirteenth-century Florentine Palazzo Feroni-Spini as his headquarters, a sign to all of his new prosperity.

Lace-up shoe by FERRAGAMO in black antelope with padded collar, silk cord laces, and antelope tassels, 1930–35. The horn toe reinterprets a design worn by the court of Louis XV. (Ferragamo Archive, Florence.)   [47]

Navy leather pump with intricately sewn bow by GEORGETTE, mid-1930s. (The Metropolitan Museum of Art, New York. Gift of Mrs. Anthony Wilson.)   [48]

While Ferragamo's fortune was improving, Italy as a whole was undergoing a period of austerity—the result of strict economic sanctions imposed by the League of Nations after the conflict in Ethiopia in 1935. Facing a shortage of

The wedge or platform sole shoes that swept into fashion in the late thirties were hardly a new design idea; indeed they can be traced back to the traditional shoes of many cultures. In ancient Greece actors wore them to be better

Black calf wedge-heel shoe by FERRAGAMO, 1936–38, with padded horn decoration. [49]

the quality steel he had used to reinforce his shoe arches, in 1936 Ferragamo devised a sole and heel from a wedge of cork, an invention that proved ideal for the wartime economy of the next decade.

seen from the stage. The chopines of Venetian ladies spread as far as England, and in William Shakespeare's *Hamlet*, first performed in 1600, one finds the line, "Your ladyship is nearer to heaven than when I saw you last, by the altitude of a chopine."[7] In Japan, a platform shoe called the *geta* was a centuries-old tradition, and it was also popular in other parts of the East. (Japanese geishas often wore high, lacquered platforms with concealed

the cork sole; in 1938 he decorated the cork sole in red velvet with rhinestones lining a tracery of embossed brass. Cedric of Paris offered high platform evening shoes covered in pink satin.

Although platforms were becoming

Laced woven-hemp shoe by FERRAGAMO, 1936–38, with three-part wooden heel covered in suede. (Ferragamo Archive, Florence.) [50]

bells that tinkled as they walked.)

The platform shoes in the late thirties were made of fine and luxurious materials. In 1936 Ferragamo created a platform sandal with a mosaic of gilded glass glued to waxed canvas covering

fashionable in Paris, when Vivier proposed a platform *à la chinoise* for New York in 1937, Herman Delman wired back, "Are you crazy?" Undaunted, Vivier presented the model to Schiaparelli, who showed it with her collec-

tion—the first of many Parisian couturiers who chose Vivier's shoes to underscore the silhouette of their creations. Perugia also designed a number of platform shoes for Schiaparelli in 1938, including a model in gold crepe rubber, a leather ankle boot with a slight platform, and a cork-soled evening shoe called a footstool, which was based on the Venetian chopines, as well as Arab wedge shoes that Schiaparelli brought back from Tunisia.

With the shortage of leather for shoe uppers in the early forties, Ferragamo turned to hemp, cellophane (transparent paper coated in plastic and strengthened by plaiting), and raffia made locally by Florentine artisans. These ingenious models received wide press attention and were acclaimed for their "interesting aesthetic quality." The transparent cellophane gave the shoe "an iridescent, almost crystalline quality; the colors [were] woven together with an original and artistic sense."[8] Once again Ferragamo showed how available materials could be used to artistic advantage.

As the war effort grew, millions of women stepped into dungarees and overalls to work in fields, munitions fac-

Two sandals by FERRAGAMO, 1935–36, with platform soles and wedge heels—left, cork sole covered in gilded glass, trimmed in gold kid and black satin; right, painted wooden sole, divided to facilitate movement, with strips of red suede. (Ferragamo Archive, Florence.)   [51–52]

*V*IVIER *exploring form by draping fabric around a woman's foot, an archetypal image of the sculptural working method of Vivier, who to this day maintains that his art is that of the sculptor. Portrait by Brassai, the foremost photographer of nocturnal Paris in the 1930s. (Roger Vivier, Paris.)* [53]

*D*rawing by VIVIER *of platform sandal, 1937, with uppers of mauve and violet jersey and a cork sole beaded with gold medallions representing the sun—a model shown by Schiaparelli. Pen on paper. (Roger Vivier, Paris.)* [54]

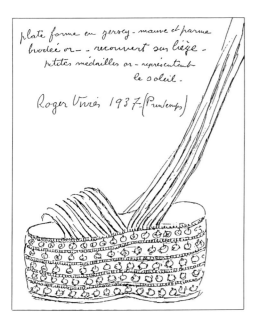

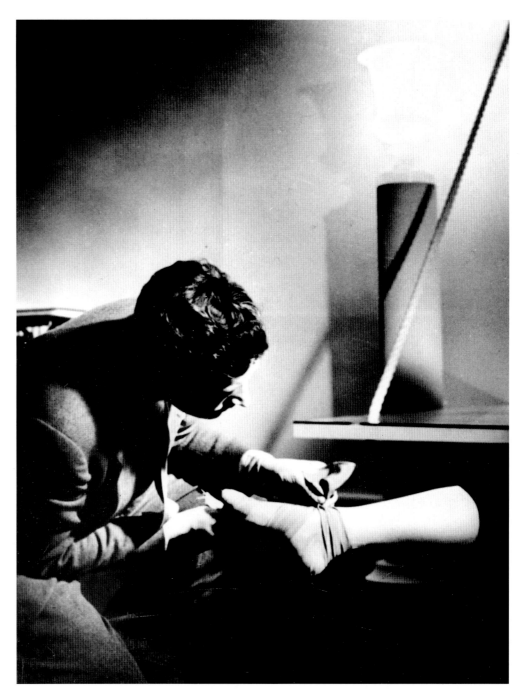

Left, suede and kidskin platform boot by PERUGIA under the "Padova" label, 1938–39; *right*, woven raffia boot by PERUGIA, c. 1939–40, in shocking pink, both probably for Schiaparelli. (Musée des Arts de la Mode, Paris. Collection of Union des Arts Décoratifs.) [55–56]

Late 1930s suede and patent leather chopine by PERUGIA, probably for Schiaparelli. (Musée Charles Jourdan, Romans.) [57]

Two FERRAGAMO evening sandals, 1940—
left, fluted cork sole covered in gold kidskin
with black satin uppers; below, sole comprised of
three layers of cork covered in kidskin and Bakelite, with a cylindrical heel of Bakelite.
(Ferragamo Archive, Florence.)   [58–59]

tories, and a million jobs left open by men who had joined the armed forces. "The Forties, reaping the bitter fruits of the previous decade, meant austerity—in dress, food, and a thousand other niggling restrictions that made life awkward," one writer has observed.[9] After 1940 wedge shoes, fabricated with wood, wool, cork, raffia, string, linen, and various fabrics, became a necessity for day and evening on both sides of the Atlantic. R. R. Bunting of London and Paris offered polished-wood platform soles with fabric uppers to accom-

pany the utility suits popular in Britain, as well as the fuller skirts seen in France. Diana Vreeland recalls that in Paris, "Everyone was in wooden shoes. *Clack clack clack.* You could tell the time of day by the sound of the wooden soles on the pavement. If there was a great storm of them, it meant that it was lunch hour and people were leaving their offices for the restaurants. Then there would be another great clatter when they returned to the office, etc. etc."[10]

In occupied France outrageous fash-

Crocheted cellophane sandal by FERRAGAMO, 1941–42, with three-layer cork heel covered in kidskin. (Ferragamo Archive, Florence.) [60]

In Italy in the early 1940s, heels and soles were made from Bakelite and plastic resins, transparent materials that served as an esthetically interesting austerity measure. Here, FERRAGAMO looks through a plastic "crystal-soled" shoe. [61]

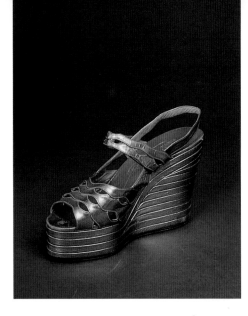

*R*ight, platform sandal in gold kidskin by GEORGETTE from the early 1940s. (Musée des Arts de la Mode, Paris. Collection of Union des Arts Décoratifs.) [62]

*B*elow left, wool felt boot with wooden sole by GEORGETTE, c. 1941–44; below right, anonymous shoe with fabric uppers and cantilevered wooden platform sole made in wartime Paris. (Left, Musée des Arts de la Mode, Paris. Collection of Union des Arts Décoratifs. Right, Musée de la Mode et du Costume, Paris.) [63–64]

ion statements soon became a form of political dissent. Women wore enormous homemade hats decorated with string, wood shavings, whatever was available. After observing the austere, utilitarian fashions in Britain, Lee Miller, a wartime reporter and photographer for *Vogue*, was intrigued by the French women's full skirts with tiny waists: "The French women deliberately organized this style of dressing as a taunt to the Huns, whose women, dressed in grey uniforms, were known as the *souris gris* [grey mice]. If the Germans cropped their hair, the French grew theirs long. If three yards of material were specified for a dress, they found fifteen for the skirt alone. Saving material and labor meant help to the Germans—and it was their duty to waste instead of save."[11] (One can see here the seeds of the full-skirted postwar "New Look.")

Highly inventive shoes continued to be produced from the available materials by Perugia, Georgette, Di Mauro, and other designers. Perugia's continuing renown is evidenced by the rumor that when the staff of the German general Rommel was frantically searching Paris to inform him of the Allied landing at Normandy, he was found at Perugia's shop, ordering shoes for a lady friend.[12]

Vivier, after serving briefly with the French forces, left for New York to work with Delman. There, he turned his talents to creating hats, an activity that widened his experimentation with fabrics and decoration, and fueled the fantasy aspect of his creations.

After the bombing of Pearl Harbor in 1941 severe restrictions were placed on shoe design in the United States, making footwear one of the most regulated industries of the wartime economy. The 1942 measures outlawed styles that required an excessive amount of leather as well as new patterns, a ruling that tolled the death knell for the shoe pattern industry.[13] (The stifling effect of these rulings on creativity paved the way for more imaginative shoes from Italy to enter the U.S. market after the war.) That same year restrictions were also placed on women's clothing, limiting pockets, wide lapels, ruffles, and skirt lengths and circumferences.

Rationing was instituted in February 1943, on a Sunday to avoid a run on merchandise in the stores. Each person was allowed only three pairs of leather shoes per year, but coupons could be transferred within a family. Some fashionable women managed to get around the quotas, and there were reports of shoe coupon sales on the black market.

Stylish cork wedge shoe by DI MAURO, late 1930s, covered with leather and finely woven raffia. (Di Mauro, Paris.)   [65]

American silver leather by the firm I. MILLER, 1942, with metal beads—an exhibition model inspired by Turkish women's silver-covered wooden platforms. (The Metropolitan Museum of Art, New York. Gift of I. Miller & Sons, Inc.) [66]

Fabric shoes were not rationed although sneakers were not available because of a rubber shortage. Consumers, restricted in their shoe purchases, reacted by buying better-quality shoes. In spite of the rationing, the war years were a boom time for the American shoe industry, which supplied great quantities of boots to the American and Allied soldiers.

Women gained a new independence from a wide variety of roles they played during the war. Winston Churchill, ad-

DI MAURO samples showing what was forbidden (right) and permitted (left) in terms of leather usage in wartime Paris, 1943. (Di Mauro, Paris.) [67]

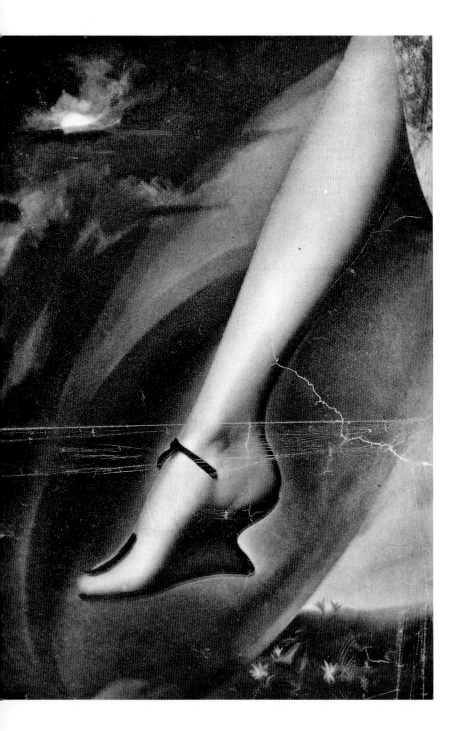

FERRAGAMO's *"Invisible Shoe"* of 1947, an F-shaped, wooden wedge heel covered in red calf with clear nylon uppers; on the left, a sketch from Il Mattino illustrato, *April 20, 1947.* *(Ferragamo Archive, Florence.)* [68–69]

dressing a gathering of six thousand women in 1943, declared, "This war effort could not have been achieved if the women had not marched forward in millions and undertaken all kinds of tasks for which any other generation but our own would have considered them unfitted....the bounds of women's activities have been definitely, vastly and permanently enlarged."[14] On the design front, fashion moved toward durable, practical styles created for comfort and

Two postwar American platform models—in black suede with red snakeskin from MACKEY STARR and green leather from NEWTON-ELKIN. (The Metropolitan Museum of Art, New York. Gift of The Guild of Better Shoe Manufacturers, Inc.) [71]

A refined postwar platform, c. 1949, by Joseph CASALE of Paris, a style that often accompanied the "New Look" fashions. (Musée de la Mode et du Costume, Paris.) [72]

ease of mobility. Claire McCardell, the American sportswear designer, offered flats and low-heeled shoes to accompany her inventive clothes for the active woman. She also introduced significant alternatives to the wedge shoe with her ballet-style flats for Capezio in 1944 and her flat-soled fabric shoes in 1945 for I. Miller.

After years of wearing sensible, comfort-oriented shoes, women now possessed beautifully formed foot carriages, something unknown to fashionable women for centuries. Platform soles and durably constructed shoes with heavy and medium-sized heels were worn well into the next decade, although sandal-type dress shoes began to take hold, signaling the arrival of the narrower heels of the fifties—a time when, for many women, comfort once again took a back seat to glamour.

CHAPTER THREE

The Triumph of the Stiletto

Stiletto pumps in black leather, late fifties or early sixties, by COVER GIRL, a London shop that offered fetish footwear from the late 1940s through the early 1980s. (Billyboy, Paris.) [73]

I don't know who invented the high heel. But all women owe him a lot.
—Marilyn Monroe[1]

High heels have long been acknowledged to have a sensual effect on women's gait and physique; indeed wherever high heels have marched across the map of history they seem to have produced a ripple of nervous and slightly scandalized reaction. A seventeenth-century decree of the British Parliament reads, "Any woman who, through the use of high heeled shoes or other devices, leads a subject of Her Majesty into marriage, shall be punished with the penalties of witchery."[2] During the French Revolution, heels on shoes disappeared altogether in reaction against high versions, which were viewed, along with powder, corsets, and hoop skirts, as the foremost symbols of the aristocracy's decadence.

But high heels were far too popular to be banished altogether, and throughout Europe these dramatic if uncomfortably vertiginous models continued to be produced over the centuries in a variety of styles. Finally, in the mid-fifties, a high heel was introduced that was more elegantly tapered and narrower than any heel before—the stiletto. While platform soles, thigh-high boots, and other shoe fashions had a long history, the stiletto was a uniquely twentieth-century creation. Isolated forerunners can be found earlier in the century in the realms of high-fashion and fetish footwear, but the stiletto heel that appeared around 1955 became an international phenomenon and a preeminent symbol of the period.

The stiletto represented a gradual refinement of a high, increasingly narrow heel made by a number of designers in Italy and in Paris between 1948 and

Early eighteenth-century French shoe with high "fishtail" heel. (Musée de la Chaussure, Romans.) [74]

High heel by PERUGIA, c. 1948, designed for a Parisian music hall revue. (Musée Charles Jourdan, Romans.) [75]

*R*ight, *FERRAGAMO, 1950, with the lasts for some of his most famous clients; on the far right, Anna Magnani getting an arch fitting for one of Ferragamo's high-heeled strappy sandals.* [76–77]

1955. Ferragamo's legendary wedge sole disappeared after 1948, and Italy, having made a remarkably rapid economic recovery after the war, stepped into the shoe market with a sandal sporting a minimum of strap and a high, delicate heel—a shoe that provided an ideal accompaniment to the resurgence of ultra-feminine clothing in Paris after the war, most notably that of Christian Dior. Introduced in 1947, Dior's "New Look" featured full, ankle-length skirts made of extravagant amounts of fabric that signaled an improvement in the postwar economy— and coincidentally drew attention to the feet and ankles. Sensing the shift in mood, shoe designers in other countries were quick to follow Italy's lead, among them, Russell Bromley in England, Bally of Switzerland, and Delman and Saks Fifth Avenue in New York. They produced the lightweight, strappy sandals that became the new glamour symbols for movie stars and fashionable women everywhere.

Ferragamo did much to promote Italian style during this era; only two years after the war he was turning out three hundred and fifty pairs of hand-produced shoes per day for export all over the world. By now he had achieved interna-

Top left, beechwood high heel from Charles JORDAN of Paris, 1951–52, with a substantial base. (Beth and Herbert Levine, New York.) [78]

Top right, sandal from VIVIER's first collection for Christian Dior, 1953. (Roger Vivier, Paris.) [79]

Bottom left, design by VIVIER of the coronation shoes for Elizabeth II, 1953, created in association with the English manufacturers Rayne. The gold kidskin sandal had a slight platform for comfort (since the Queen remained standing during the three-hour ceremony) and a heel studded with garnets. Pen and pencil on paper. (Roger Vivier, Paris.) [80]

Bottom right, black satin evening pumps by VIVIER for Dior, 1953–55, with rhinestone-ball heel of almost stiletto narrowness—a style worn by Marlene Dietrich. (Katell le Bourhis, New York.) [81]

Violà, the stiletto—on the left, VIVIER's talon aiguille, or "needle" heel, 1955, compared with JORDAN's more substantial heel, 1951–52. (Left: Roger Vivier, Paris. Right: Beth and Herbert Levine, New York.) [82–83]

tional acclaim with a clientele that included Greta Garbo (who during one visit ordered seventy pairs), as well as Anna Magnani and Sophia Loren, two Italian screen actresses with very different images who both wore high heels by Ferragamo.

Although the term *stiletto heel* was first used in 1953, the Italian high heels at this time were not yet as finely tapered as the true stiletto heel.[3] In 1955 Vivier, working in association with Dior, introduced two stunning new designs: *talon choc* and *talon aiguille* (the "shock" and "needle" heels).[4] The needle heel was finely tapered and reinforced with steel—a heel now so commonplace that it is difficult to conceive just how daring it was. The shock heel had an equally narrow arc of curved steel, and both silhouettes were completed by the pointy toes soon known as needle toes.

Although it is difficult to prove who made it first, Vivier is generally credited with creating the stiletto heel, for he presented the most inventive array of elegantly tapered models with the most

Talon choc, or "shock" heel, another of VIVIER's elegant and precise heels, shown here on a deliriously embroidered evening sandal for Dior, c. 1955–57—a startling silouette finished with a turned-up toe. (The Metropolitan Museum of Art, New York. Gift of Valerian Stux-Rybar.) [84]

Beaded stiletto pump from DAL CO of Rome, c. 1955. (The Metropolitan Museum of Art, New York. Gift of Nives Dalco.) [85]

Brown leather stiletto sandal by ALBANESE of Rome, mid-fifties. (The Metropolitan Museum of Art, New York. Gift of Margaret Jerrold, Inc.) [86]

distinctive silhouettes. Yet that same year, 1955, a trend was noted in Italy toward higher and thinner heels on models shown by Albanese and Dal Co in Rome. Even Ferragamo, who insisted on comfort as the hallmark of his style, offered a number of stiletto models in 1955–56, but with a rounder toe that provided the extra room his arch fittings required. Voilà—the stiletto heel as we know it.

With worldwide attention focused on Dior creations at the time—and thereby on the shoes Vivier designed for his collections—as well as the growing interest in Italian shoes, the popularity of the stiletto heel spread far and wide. Unfortunately the early heels broke easily, especially in lower-quality models, but soon stilettos were made by encasing a metal spigot in plastic, a technique still widely used today. Then another impediment arose: officials discovered that stilettos were damaging to floors and soon they were banned from many public buildings as well as airplanes. One young man recalls that his mother once stepped on the bathroom scale in stiletto pumps and punctured it with two tiny holes.

Magazine and newspaper articles warned of the dangers of high heels, as they had in the 1930s and at the turn of the century. In England one foot specialist, citing the continuous effort to counter the forward thrust of the body, noted that wearing three-inch heels expended two and a half times more energy than walking on lower heels. He also decried what he called "juvenile shoe delinquency," charging that "teenagers, too, are becoming addicts of court shoes, pencil-heeled with toes as sharp as the fangs of the biblical serpent."[5]

By the end of the fifties pointed toes had become so extreme that some women bought shoes two sizes too large to accommodate their toes, and it was rumored that others had their smallest toes removed to better fit the fashion. While this was probably an isolated occurrence, at least one account survives of a young woman who had to have a toe removed after wearing the "currently fashionable boots." According to her doctor's cynical report, she was delighted because she could now wear her boots one size smaller.[6] "If women want needle toes they must be prepared to pay the consequences," warned the dismayed English foot specialist, illustrating his point with X rays of cramped toes and hammer toes, and citing bunions and thickened ankles.[7]

In Hollywood, stiletto heels became

an important element in creating the images of Jayne Mansfield, who owned more than two hundred pairs; Anita Ekberg, who slipped off her embroidered stiletto pumps to frolic in the Trevi fountain in *La Dolce Vita;* and Marilyn Monroe, who noted that the high heel in general had "given a lift" to her career.[8] These sex symbols were also instrumental in putting women into uplift bras, pencil-slim skirts, and other restrictive, movement-inhibiting fashions of the times. Stilettos couldn't turn every woman into a sex goddess, but they did lend a certain allure. As one *Saturday Evening Post* "postscript" put it:

> The girl with low
> and sensible heels
> Is likely to pay for her
> bed and meals.[9]

One explanation for the rise of the stiletto both as fashion and as a symbol of the period was that it embodied, quite literally, society's efforts to put women back on the pedestal. At the end of the war an editorial in British *Vogue* raised the question, "How long before a grateful nation (or anyhow the men of a nation) forget what women accomplished when the country needed them? It's up to women to see that there

is no regression—that they go right on from here."[10] Within a few years, however, women had lost their place in the work force. Rosie the Riveter and more active role models disappeared, and once again the ideal of the male-supporter and female-homemaker became the norm.

Already sensing the changing mood in 1947, Simone de Beauvoir wrote, "Women are afraid that if they lose their feeling of inferiority, they will lose what gives them value in the eyes of men—femininity. . . . If a woman succeeds with brilliance in business, in social life, in her profession, she often suffers an inferiority complex in comparison to other women. She feels herself less charming, less agreeable. . . . Either women renounce in part the integration of their personalities or they abandon in part their power of seduction over men."[11] In the fifties, as women lost power in other spheres of activity, they could slip on a pair of stiletto heels to enhance their seductiveness and feel that they still had some power over men.

Stilettos both symbolized and helped effect the subjugation of women, but both sexes seemed to derive a fair amount of enjoyment from them. Women willingly conspired to wear stiletto heels, which rendered them virtually im-

Needle-toe pump by the Italian designer
MIRO ABBA, illustrated in Abba's catalog,
1963–64. (The Metropolitan Museum of Art,
New York. Costume Institute Library.) [87]

Black patent fetish pump by anonymous
maker, with red patent heel seven inches high. In
the West, fetish footwear has almost always been
slick, hard-edged, and weaponlike, while in
Eastern cultures it reminds one more of lingerie,
with satin uppers and sometimes delicately embroidered soles. (Musée de la Chaussure,
Romans.) [88]

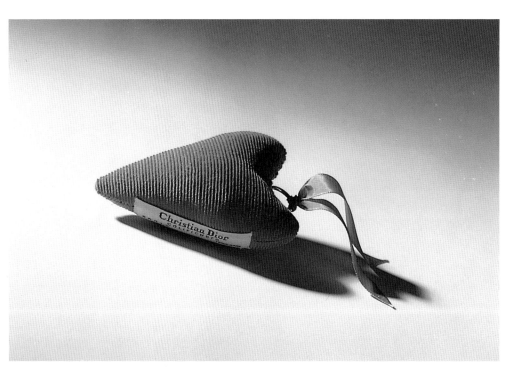

Luxurious pad with DIOR label to preserve
the shoe's delicate toe shape. (Billyboy,
Paris.) [89]

Narrow pointed-toe silhouette typical of
VIVIER's high heels for Dior in the fifties.
(Roger Vivier, Paris.) [90]

mobile beyond short distances. Some women simply liked the way the heels made them look and they knew this look was pleasing to men. No matter how finely crafted or well balanced they were, any shoe that jimmied the foot up at such an angle hurt, but the pain didn't seem to matter. Interestingly, studies have indicated that many men, even those who are not foot fetishists, find it sexually exciting just to hear a woman reveal that she is wearing painful shoes.[12]

The repressive climate of the fifties supported a healthy crop of underground fetish magazines. Nearly all of them gave substantial coverage to shoe fetishes, which interested a major segment of their audience. *Fantastique*, published by Sheba, was strictly pictorial while *Exotique*, published by Burmel, offered articles on the history of corsets and fantasies of a shoe salesman. These digest-sized reviews showed some of the most outrageous fetish shoes ever created. One photograph pictured a pair of boots styled to give the impression that the feet were nearly vertical, as if the wearer were toe-dancing in ballet slippers. These were boots for bondage, models definitely not meant for walking or even maintaining an upright position.

What exactly shoe fetishists do—their rituals of pain and pleasure—is recounted in great detail in William Rossi's *Sex Life of the Foot and Shoe*. Let it suffice here to note the experience of one fetishist, N., who revealed his fantasies in the French weekly *Union*: "My shoes constitute a harem of which I am the sultan. Each shoe has a feminine name. When I choose one shoe as my partner, I often place two or others nearby as voyeurs."[13] It is impossible to say how many shoe fetishists there are since it is not usually an openly admitted desire. Clearly, however, it is still a thriving fascination; according to Rossi, London boasts an establishment called the Palace of Pedic Pleasure, one of the international circuit of brothels offering specialized services for foot and shoe fetishists. And in 1984 the French *Elle* reported on a shoe collector's club with two hundred members, sixty percent male, who collected shoes and stockings from the fifties and sixties, which they considered to be truly the most erotic.[14]

Vivian Infantino, the Fashion Director of *Footwear News*, recalls that the high-heeled "bitchy pump" became a symbol of the fifties; in black suede with a pointy toe it was "possibly the biggest single shoe look of the 1950s."[15] But of course not all women in the fifties

Below, red ballet toe shoes worn by Moira Shearer in the film The Red Shoes, *1948. (Northampton Museums and Art Gallery, Northampton, England.)* [91]

The astonishing boots on the right gave the impression that the wearer's feet were almost vertical; far right, the cocktail shaker look. Makers of fetish models relished the extreme and ignored fashion trends, as shown here by these platforms from the mid-fifties, an era when platforms were not actually popular. [92–93]

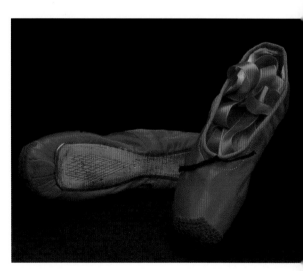

adopted the highly erotic stiletto look. Eleanor Roosevelt, typical of the woman who preferred fit and comfort over style, continued to have her shoes made by an orthopedic shoemaker in Massachusetts. And Audrey Hepburn chose Ferragamo's low-heeled styles over his stiletto models. Rossi notes that along with more suggestive labels such as Pussycat, Caressa, and Risqué, there were also companies appealing to a different clientele—Red Cross, Arch Relief, Foot Defender, and Life Stride. Flat-heeled ballet slippers were worn with long, swingy skirts, and tennis shoes were widely adopted by both sexes. In 1957 Chanel reintroduced her two-tone sling, fabricated by Massaro

of Paris—a shoe that, like her suits, offered a more comfort-minded alternative that continues to be widely copied today. By the late fifties all sorts of mini-heels, including low and medium heels by the American designer Margaret Jerrold, became popular, although these shoes still very often had pointed toes.

Even though the stiletto heel was incredibly popular, it was only one among many heels and new silhouettes created by Vivier and other designers in the fifties. For Vivier in particular, this was an era of unbridled invention. He joined the house of Dior in January 1953, a time when all eyes in the fashion world were on Dior and each collection made international news. His ten-year associ-

Striking silhouette from 1954–55: violet suede and gold kidskin mule with partial wedge, a comfort-minded shoe that was one of FERRAGAMO's last wedge designs. (Ferragamo Archive, Florence.) [94]

Two-toned sling back shoe, fabricated by Massaro of Paris, designed and worn by Coco CHANEL, late fifties; on the right, an illustration of Mademoiselle Chanel by Cecil Beaton showing the importance of the shoe to the Chanel look. (Shoe: Northampton Museums and Art Gallery, Northampton, England.)   [95–96]

Black suede pump by Margaret JERROLD, 1959–60. (The Metropolitan Museum of Art, New York. Gift of Margaret Jerrold, Inc.) [97]

ation with the house marked a golden era in shoe design. Until Dior's death in 1957, the two designers worked together closely, and Vivier became the only person to enjoy the privilege of being Dior's cosignatory. Dresses inspired shoes and sometimes vice versa, with Vivier suggesting lines and materials to Dior that would work well with his shoes.[16]

Vivier, who did not come from a shoemaking family, had always conceived of shoes in terms of fashion. His musings on the character of the silhouette, for example, inspired a wealth of new heels, including one made from a ball of rhinestones; another called the *bobine* or spool heel; the comma heel of 1959, a tour de force of curved steel developed with the assistance of aeronautics engineers; and the Louis XV heel, an interpretation of a historical model that curved inward, terminating almost at the center of the shoe.

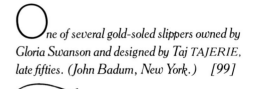

One of several gold-soled slippers owned by Gloria Swanson and designed by Taj TAJERIE, late fifties. (John Badum, New York.) [99]

Window at Tiffany's with peacock-feather shoe by Beth LEVINE, 1958, specially commissioned to accompany Jean Schlumberger's precious jewelry. [98]

"Christian Dior crée par Roger VIVIER," 1956–57, with embroidery by Rébé and talon aiguille. (*The Metropolitan Museum of Art, New York. Gift of Valerian Stux-Rybar.*)   [100]

Blue satin evening shoe by VIVIER for Dior, 1957–63. (The Metropolitan Museum of Art, New York. Gift of Valerian Stux-Rybar.) [101]

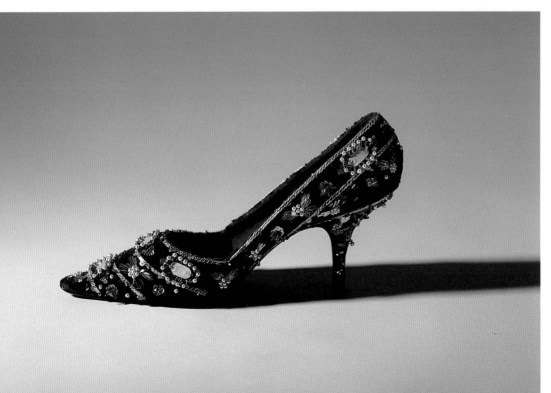

Purple velvet silhouette by VIVIER for Dior, c. 1958, with iridescent sequins and beads. (The Metropolitan Museum of Art, New York. Gift of Valerian Stux-Rybar.) [102]

Thinking in terms of décolleté, Vivier also created marvelous toes: squared off, pointed, turned up—always the height of elegance. Even the soles of his shoes were lyrically shaped. The underside of one form, which he named "Mandoline," suggests a guitar silhouette.

While the craftsmanship employed to create many of the Dior-Vivier models was virtually uncopyable, the shapes offered were widely imitated. Vivier maintains that his designs have always

been "simple, with a balance of seriousness and fantasy."[17] Still, while the line may have been masterfully pure, it was not unusual during his years with Dior for a shoe to be completely embroidered with pearls or feathers, or for an enchantingly spare pump to have crystal beads cascading down the back of the heel. Working with the renowned French embroiderers Rébé, Vivier created fantastically ornate shoes in tulle, lace, and rhinestones, which were sought after by such fashionable women

A *divine repertoire of toes and a multitude of innovative heels by VIVIER for Dior, late fifties. (Both photos: Roger Vivier, Paris, and The Metropolitan Museum of Art, New York. Gift of Valerian Stux-Rybar.) [103–4]*

*B*lack suede pump with talon choc, *1960, la-beled "Christian Dior, Roger VIVIER, Paris."* *(Musée des Arts de la Mode, Paris. Collection of Union Française des Arts du Costume.)* [105]

Fake fur slipper by VIVIER for Dior, 1962, with mini-heel. (The Metropolitan Museum of Art, New York. Gift of Valerian Stux-Rybar.) [106]

as Patricia Lopez (who with her husband Arturo gave the most elegant Parisian balls of the fifties) and Princess Grace of Monaco (who ordered scores of Vivier's extraordinarily crafted shoes to complement her Dior gowns). Diana Vreeland once placed an embroidered evening shoe by Vivier alongside an or-

nate eighteenth-century French shoe and declared that "the level of quality was identical."[18]

These gorgeous creations demanded a certain respect. Shoes so delicate and precious needed pampering, as a woman found who once purchased a pair of Vivier's rapturously embroi-

84

dered, very steep stiletto pumps, the most ornate of the season's collection. She returned the following day with the beadwork slightly torn, complaining that the shoes were uncomfortable. After examining the soles, the boutique's manager Michel Brodsky responded—just as Empress Josephine's shoemaker was said to have replied when her delicate slippers developed a hole after only one wearing—"But, Madame, you *walked* in these shoes."[19]

During his first two years with Dior, Vivier was still under contract with Delman and so his label from 1953 to 1955 read "Delman, Christian Dior, Paris." After two years of made-to-measure shoes, Vivier and Dior launched a ready-to-wear line, "Christian Dior crée par Roger Vivier, Paris," fabricated by Charles Jourdan. This was the first time a couturier had associated his label with a bottier for such a venture, a precedent that has been widely followed.

In the mid- to late fifties the Italian

V̶IVIER's evocation of the red slippers of Marcel Proust's Duchesse de Guermantes, for Dior, 1963. (Roger Vivier, Paris.)   [107]

$\mathcal{P}$ink and green satin sandal by VIVIER for Dior, late fifties or early sixties. (The Metropolitan Museum of Art, New York. Gift of Valerian Stux-Rybar.) [108]

$\mathcal{E}$vening pump by VIVIER for Dior, 1960, in kingfisher feathers with talon choc. (The Metropolitan Museum of Art, New York. Gift of Valerian Stux-Rybar.) [109]

*C*heckered fabric pump, a striking silhouette
by *VIVIER*, 1961. (Roger Vivier,
Paris.) [110]

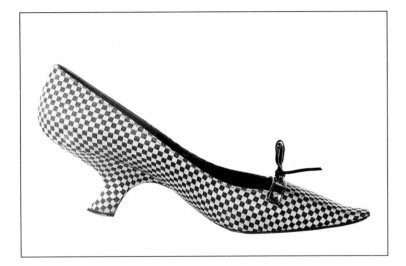

*S*hoe designed by Pablo PICASSO and fabricated by Perugia, late fifties. A small number were made as promotional items, this one given to an official in the French Ministry of Culture. (Christian Louboutin, Paris.) [111]

Two from PERUGIA: leather sandal with a metal arc heel, c. 1955, and a pump with a coil-like heel, possibly early fifties. Although these are two of the latest models by Perugia in museum collections, a number of sources note that he worked in Paris until 1970. (Musée Charles Jourdan, Romans.)   [112–13]

shoe industry began to gain ground in the American market. In 1957 U.S. footwear imports exceeded exports for the first time, with Italy providing the high-quality shoes and Japan filling in the lower end of the market.[20] But stylistically Italy was an even greater influence than the import figures indicate, and American manufacturers began keeping a close eye on Italian designers. "Italy leads the world in shoe creativity. The same art that France puts into its clothes, Italy puts into its shoes," reported Charline Osgood, an American who was sent to Europe to scout shoe trends between 1954 and 1958 for several American shoe companies. Osgood pointed to a "modern functionalism" in shoe design, citing Charles Jourdan and Durer in Paris, Albanese and Dal Co in Rome, and Mauri of Florence for their "design integrity, fine craftsmanship, and simplicity."[21] By the end of the fifties, however, it had become increasingly difficult for shoe designers to find artisans skilled in the craft of shoemaking. As Ferragamo noted, "The machine age was advancing remorselessly. The crafts of handmade shoes no longer appealed to youth."[22]

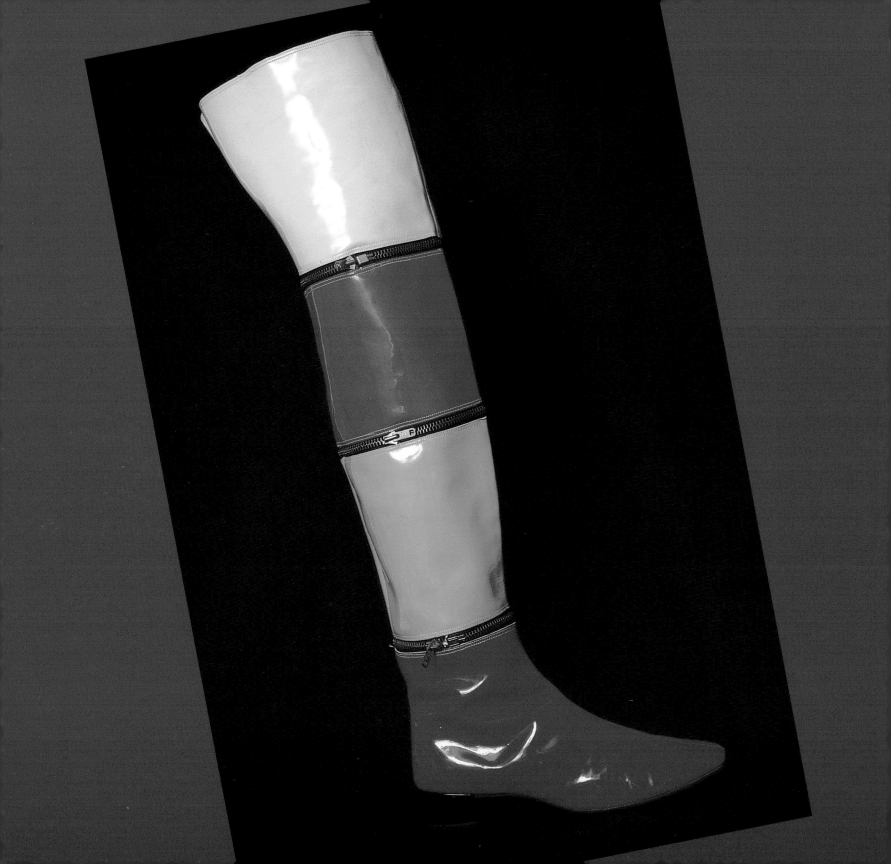

CHAPTER FOUR

Youthquake

These boots are made for walkin' . . .
—Nancy Sinatra[1]

In the early sixties the attitude toward clothing fashion began to merge compatibly with machine-made footwear. The emphasis was no longer on well-made clothes but on cheap chic, a throwaway esthetic in which plastic and paper replaced silk and satin as the fashion fabrics. Exuberant images of youth abounded in fashion magazines in an ever-accelerating quick-change of styles. Street looks began to inspire high fashion, and the concept of owning a couture "original" lost its cachet. Brigitte Bardot declared that couture was for grandmothers, and Yves Saint Laurent pronounced it "passé," opening his first Rive Gauche ready-to-wear boutique in 1965.

The sixties ushered in a more popu-list era of fashion. While pop art was reevaluating the "beauty" of everyday objects, the fashion world was redefining elegance in terms as far removed as possible from the complacent conservatism of the fifties' feminine ideal. The ethnic styles, secondhand clothing, and mass-produced fashions worn by the hippies had a tremendous influence, signaling a rejection of the materialism and middle-class values of the fifties. The civil rights movement, women's liberation, and later, resistance to the Vietnam War—all worked together to forge an influential counterculture that questioned high culture in all its manifestations. And the fashion world responded. In the mid-sixties, for example, as black became beautiful, the first black models appeared in the glossy fashion magazines and a new interest arose in African-inspired fashions.

Like clothing, shoe fashions took a

Adjustable-height boot by the American company GOLO, 1967, in patent leather and rubber with multiple zippers. (The Metropolitan Museum of Art, New York. Gift of the Golo Footwear Corporation.) [114]

completely different turn from the pointed toes and stiletto heels that had spelled elegance in the previous decade. A vast selection of low and moderate heels appeared. By 1964 Vivier and Charles Jourdan were showing broader toes, both round and square, which were widely copied. Some shoes were even styled to resemble Mary Janes, with rounded toes and a strap across the front, the perfect accompaniment to the little-girl fashions that, as the magazines proclaimed, could be worn by women of all ages who sported a youthful attitude.

Shoe materials also underwent changes. Plastic "wet-look" finishes and other synthetics complemented the "space-age" look promoted by fashion designer André Courrèges. Clear plastic shoes by Herbert Levine, Vivier, I. Miller, and others came into vogue. "Mock croc" was fashionable after 1963, when Saint Laurent showed thigh-high crocodile boots by Vivier. Fake became fabulous as synthetic materials pervaded all aspects of daily life.

And then there was the miniskirt, exposing an expanse of leg and ushering in a craze for boots of all heights. Such leggy models as Penelope Tree, Jean Shrimpton, Twiggy, and Veruschka romped across the fashion pages, while two of the main designers of the mini

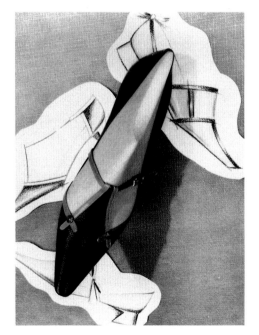

Patent leather pump by Charles JOURDAN, 1965, with a mini-heel and rounded toe. (Musée Charles Jourdan, Romans.) [115]

Sketch for mini-heel T-strap by Miro ABBA, 1966. (The Metropolitan Museum of Art, New York. Costume Institute Library.) [116]

Leather and plastic souliers de cristal by
VIVIER, early sixties. (Roger Vivier,
Paris.) [117]

Clear plastic shoes by Herbert LEVINE,
early sixties. (Billyboy, Paris.) [118]

look—Mary Quant in London and André Courrèges in Paris—did much to promote ankle- and knee-high boots. In 1964 Courrèges showed knee-high, white patent leather boots with cutaway panels and squarish toes for day and completely sequined models for evening. The next year Quant offered ankle boots of injection-molded plastic (a fabrication technique first employed in Britain in 1956), which proved suitable for English rainy days. The clear plastic low heel was stamped with a flower, the Quant trademark.

Vivier set the trend for thigh-high *cuissarde* boots with a fashion boot based on chausses, a traditional item of male clothing over the centuries. (One of the charges brought against Joan of Arc in 1431 was that she had worn them.) Although *cuissardes* had been created earlier for fetish footwear, it was only in the sixties, when Vivier designed them for the lithesome legs of the dancers Zizi Jeanmarie and Rudolf Nureyev, that they became a fashion trend. Vivier made them in black leather for

Thigh-high crocodile boots by *VIVIER*, c. *1965, for Yves Saint Laurent.*   [119]

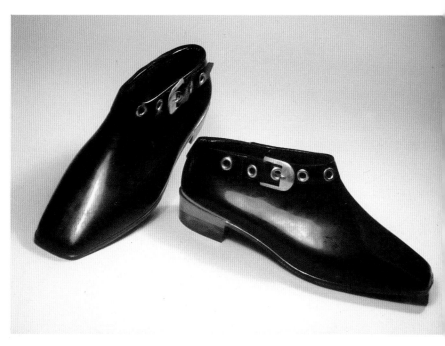

Injection-molded plastic ankle boots by Mary QUANT, 1965, with fabric lining. (Bata Shoe Museum Foundation, Toronto.)   [121]

Plastic boots by André COURRÈGES, 1964, with original box. (Bata Shoe Museum Foundation, Toronto.)   [120]

S*tacked and rolled heels by Herbert*
LEVINE, mid-sixties. (Beth and Herbert
Levine, New York.)   [122]

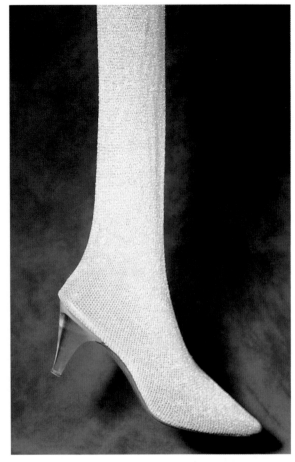

O*ne of many versions of the LEVINE stretch*
boot, 1967. (Beth and Herbert Levine, New
York.)   [123]

*P*atent leather and vinyl sports-car shoe designed by Katherine DENZINGER for Herbert Levine, 1965. (The Metropolitan Museum of Art, New York. Gift of Herbert Levine, Inc.) [124]

Brigitte Bardot, who wore them astride a Harley Davidson motorcycle in a music film clip, singing a song by Serge Gainsbourg.

Some of the most provocative designs of the sixties came from the American shoe designers Beth and Herbert Levine. They offered stacked and rolled heels as well as shoes exhibiting a pop influence that resembled a sports car or Aladdin's lamp. In 1967 they designed their most influential model, the stretch boot, for which they won a Coty Award. Soon after they showed pantyhose boots with clear acrylic heels and

even an all-in-one design with pants and boots connected.

In Paris, Vivier continued to be a major influence in the world of high-fashion footwear. Beginning in 1962–63 through 1970, he designed shoes for Yves Saint Laurent. Together, Vivier and Saint Laurent launched a model that was destined to become one of history's most copied shoes: the silver-buckle pilgrim pump first designed in 1962 to accompany Saint Laurent's "Mondrian" collection. Several versions were made—some with rounder toes, others more square, but all with a lean,

elegant silhouette. By 1965 *Footwear News* published a fashion "Honor Roll" of women wearing this status shoe, among them the duchess of Windsor, Anne Ford, Mrs. Loel Guinness, Mrs. Gianni Agnelli, Marlene Dietrich, Elsa Martinelli, and three Rothschild baronesses.[2] In the film *Belle de Jour* the surrealist film director Luis Buñuel used the pilgrim pump as a central image to establish the upper-class social position of the lead character, played by Catherine Deneuve. Even such a subdued design in Buñuel's hands could be a bit unsettling.

In 1963 Vivier opened a salon across the street from Dior, with a clientele Diana Vreeland described as "all the women who loved perfection." As she explains, "All my life I've had my shoes custom made, but only Vivier is perfection."[3] Saint Laurent offered similar praise, saying that Vivier "brought to his metier a level of charm, delicacy, refinement and poetry unsurpassed."[4] According to Vreeland, Vivier concentrated on the designing while Michel Brodsky, the manager of the shop who collaborated with Vivier for many years, "created the charm of the shop and the luxury of a two-hour fitting for one pair of shoes."[5] Brodsky indicated that the list of fashionable women who frequented the salon was endless, in-

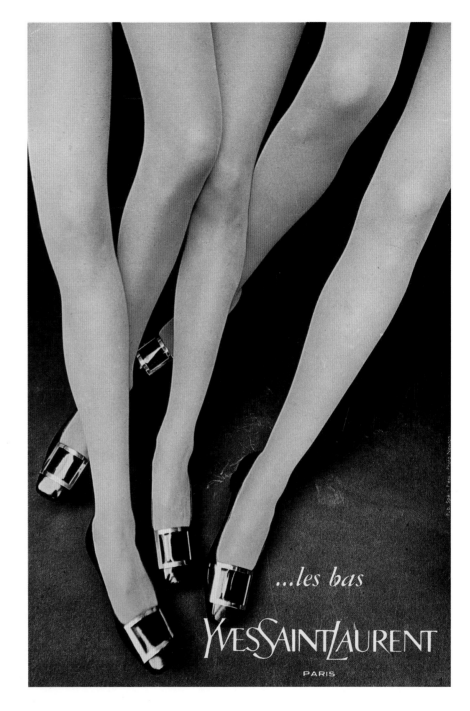

...les bas

YVESSAINTAURENT

PARIS

Ad for Yves Saint Laurent stockings featuring the pilgrim pump, c. 1964–65.   [125]

Below, pair of Diana Vreeland's satin slippers by DAL CO, mid-sixties. (Diana Vreeland, New York.)   [126]

Right, Vreeland proves that "fake is fabulous," wearing red plastic VIVIER boots printed to resemble snakeskin, late sixties.   [127]

"*Ball of diamonds*" *heel by VIVIER for Marlene Dietrich, 1967. (Roger Vivier, Paris.)* [129]

"*For all the women who loved perfection*"—*crocodile shoes by VIVIER, c. 1966, with each scale painstakingly hand-colored in a mosaic pattern. Vivier considered this to be one of his most extravagant models. (Mrs. Walter Pharr, New York.)* [128]

*S*atin platform shoe with rhinestones by *VIVIER*, 1967–68. (*Musée des Arts de la Mode, Paris. Collection of Union Française des Arts du Costume.*)   [130]

cluding Marlene Dietrich (who lived nearby and visited almost every day), Ava Gardner, Sophia Loren, Elizabeth Taylor, Gina Lollobrigida, Jacqueline Kennedy-Onassis, the Comtesse de Paris, Maria Callas, Jean Shrimpton, Empress Farah Dibah of Iran, and the Empress Nagako of Japan.[6]

Vivier continued to experiment with new heels, fabrics, and silhouettes, designing for such Parisian fashion designers as Cristobal Balenciaga, Emmanuel Ungaro, Madame Grès, and André Courrèges, as well as Saint Laurent. In 1967 he reintroduced the platform shoe, creating bejeweled platforms the following year for Jeanne Moreau in the film *La Grande Catherine.* Paloma Picasso also designed platform shoes in 1968, and before long they could once again be seen nearly everywhere.

The rage for platforms four to six inches high continued in the early seventies despite warnings from medical experts that prolonged wear could cause irrevocable damage to the spine. The Italian design house Casadei offered an inventive array of platform styles, as did

Barbara Hulanicki of Biba and Terry de Havilland in London. In 1972 Harold Smerling presented his infamous "goldfish" platforms with aquarium-like heels of glass—not a practical concept, but one widely published in the fashion press. A designer known as Mundo in Los Angeles hand-painted custom platforms for Diana Ross and Elton John. From discos to senior proms, on men and on women, platforms took over until 1978, when more refined shapes began to replace "monster shoes."

By the mid-seventies fashion had begun to branch in two directions—on one hand there were the sensible, "dress-for-success" and sportswear looks, featuring pants and practical, comfort-oriented separates, and on the other an antifashion trend became very influential in more avant-garde circles although it did not greatly affect volume

D̲I MAURO's exquisite craftsmanship is still evident in this silver loafer from the sixties. Although he died in 1988, his atelier continues to craft only custom-order footwear. (Di Mauro, Paris.) [132]

M̲od, metallic leather pumps by JOHN WRIGHT'S SWINGING LONDON GROUP. (Billyboy, Paris.) [131]

104 ～

Black leather platform fetish boots by anonymous maker, early seventies. (Billyboy, Paris.) [133]

Prototype of metallic-finish fabric platforms by BIBA of London, early seventies. (Billyboy, Paris.) [134]

sales. In line with the first trend, comfortable yet stylish loafers and moccasins were offered by countless designers and manufacturers. Gucci, for example, introduced a widely copied moccasin style in 1966; Fratelli Rossetti displayed moccasins and lace-up oxfords in a multitude of colors; and Joan Helpern of Joan & David offered flats stylish enough to be worn in a variety of contexts.

The contrasting antifashion impulse perpetuated the counterculture rejection of established values. In London, Vivienne Westwood and other designers involved with the music scene broad-

casted a strong message of social protest, wearing what might be described as "shredded chic," a tough street look that featured ripped clothes and lots of black leather. On their feet they sported sturdy Doc Martens or similar boots encrusted with buckles, metal studs, and toe caps. Another offbeat English fashion that spread west was the purposely coarse-looking rubber or crepe-soled shoe, a look that had been popular in England for men's shoes in the early fifties.

The English shoes of this period went even farther than the shoes of the sixties in creating an antithesis to the glamour shoes of the fifties. Stylishly clunky, and in many cases still quite expensive, these shoes gave women a highly comfortable but visually interesting way to accentuate a modern spirit in their dress. They announced a strong personality— here was a woman who felt secure about her looks and dressed for herself, not to please a man.

The more populist fashions of the sixties forged an image of women that stressed not just what they wore, but

Glitter platform by anonymous maker, mid-seventies. (Susanne Bartsch, New York.) [135]

The stiletto never went out of fashion for some women, and it enjoyed a revival around 1973. Here, a black patent model made in Spain for Frederick's of Hollywood, a mail-order house established in 1946 that has long been well known for its fetishistic footwear. (Susanne Bartsch, New York.) [136]

*W*edge-soled shoe by Vivienne WESTWOOD, c. 1985. (Susanne Bartsch, New York.)   [137]

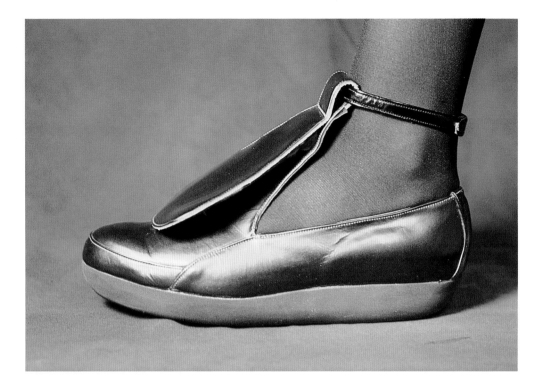

who they were. As Diana Vreeland, the influential editor-in-chief of *Vogue* from 1962 to 1971, explains, "a new dress doesn't get you anywhere; it's the life you're living in that dress."[7] In the fifties, fashion news was issued in the form of strict pronouncements that informed women of the new silhouette and the new hemline. In the sixties, however, women were encouraged to invent their own style, to "do their own thing." Fashion was about *options*, today a ubiquitous buzzword in the fashion world, just as women began to find more options in their careers and identities.

POSTSCRIPT

Carnival of Soles: Present Day Wit and Invention

A man cannot make a pair of shoes rightly unless he do it in a devout manner. —Thomas Carlyle[1]

Shoe design in the twentieth century is a visual feast with an incredible variety of memorable shoes. Yet today, the métier of the shoe designer is becoming increasingly obsolete. A designer who insists on creating his or her own shapes and heels is isolated more and more in a world of machine production. Most shoes produced in the multi-billion-dollar shoe industry are merely assembled from a selection of standard heels and lasts, a component-oriented system that explains why so many shoes these days look alike except for variations in color and detailing.

Fortunately for shoe lovers, hold-outs can still be found among shoe designers who continue to develop their own heels and lasts. But the process is costly, allowing the designer to introduce only a few new heels and silhouettes per season. Developing and correcting a last may cost thousands of dollars; likewise creating a new heel can also involve great expense, depending on how challenging the heel is to fabricate and how much experimentation is required to perfect it. In addition, any model for which the heel or last has been specially created rather than selected from the factory's stock cannot be attached by machine and must be assembled by hand, a necessity that not only allows for a more uniquely-shaped model but guarantees that the shoe is better crafted. These factors explain why the shoe designer's work today can be equated with that of the couturier, and why finer shoes cost so much.

"Marly" by VIVIER, 1986–87—a satin evening boot with rosette and Guignol heel. (Musée des Arts de la Mode, Paris. Collection of Union Française des Arts Décoratifs.) [138]

S atin evening shoes with beadwork by Manolo BLAHNIK, 1991. (Manolo Blahnik, London.) [139]

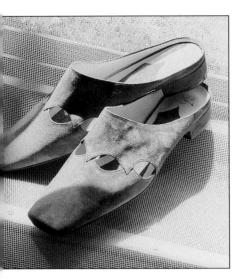

O pen-backed design in suede by Michel PERRY, 1991. [140]

S uede open-back pump by Maud FRIZON, 1988. (Maud Frizon, Paris.) [141]

"L anguette" by Christian LOUBOUTIN from the winter collection, 1991–92. (Christian Louboutin, Paris.) [142]

It has long been true that when a woman was feeling a little blue or simply wanted to spoil herself, there was no better tonic than buying a fabulous pair of shoes. But these days, the price for even a less than remarkable pair may send her from slight depression into a state of shock. Shoes priced at more than $400 are found in the shoe boutiques of Maud Frizon and Manolo Blahnik as well as in major department stores. Those prices are commanded by stylish pumps in leather and suede, nicely made but a far cry from the beautifully handcrafted shoes that were available, and not at a king's ransom, until the end of the 1950s.

Among the shoes designed today, the most memorable seem to reflect the primacy of ideas over craftsmanship, a situation that first arose in the sixties. Without the benefit of the exquisite craftsmanship that historically characterized fine shoe design—and that in all but a few cases is gone forever—designers must now rely on witty, eye-catching designs or on the beauty of a simple yet striking silhouette.

Despite the challenges inherent in the production process, an astonishing number of delightful and inventive shoes continue to be made by a great many designers, among them Robert Clergerie, Maud Frizon, Emma Hope,

Satin evening mule by Manolo BLAHNIK, 1988. (Manolo Blahnik, London.) [143]

Pen and ink drawing by Ruben TOLEDO for the decor of the shoe salon at Galeries Lafayette, which offers perhaps the best selection in New York of French shoes. (Ruben Toledo, New York.) [144]

Three models by Sarah METTLER from the summer collection, 1991. (Sarah Mettler, New York.) [145]

Stephane Kelian, Philippe Model, and Michel Perry, to name only a few. Two newcomers have also made strong showings with collections of whimsical and well-made designs. When Christian Louboutin opened his Parisian boutique in the autumn of 1991, the French press met his chic flats and elegant evening styles with a deluge of praise. And New York-based Sarah Mettler has produced an impressive number of strikingly beautiful designs in only five or six collections.

Unquestionably the prince of shoes today is Manolo Blahnik, whose devotees proclaim him to be the master of unabashed fantasy shoes and a consummate illusionist capable of making the widest foot appear chic and narrow. In film and entertainment circles, he has a great many fans, from Angelica Huston and Whitney Houston to Annette Bening, Geena Davis, Julia Roberts, and Winona Ryder. Indeed his shoes seem to lend an aura of glamour that seems otherwise

T*ri-color leather ghillie by Hermès, 1991.*
[146]

Far left, above, shapely suede model by
Elizabeth STUART-SMITH, 1988.
(Elizabeth Stuart-Smith, London.)   [147]

Far left, below, silk pump by Emma HOPE,
1988. (Emma Hope, London.)   [148]

*L*eft, *handmade leather shoe by Yona* LEVINE, *1987. (Yona Levine, New York.)* [149]

*R*ight, *"Chain Reaction," by Patrick* COX, *1988. (Patrick Cox, London.)* [150]

lacking in Hollywood these days. About Blahnik, Madonna has exulted, "His shoes are wonderful, and they last longer than sex."[2] Likewise, he himself has noted, "I've become aware of what shoes are now in this kind of modern society. Entertainment. Total entertainment. . . . Quality is always going to be paramount, but on top of that, the shoe has got to be an escape. You put a shoe on, and it's like *Cinderella.* You look down and say, How lovely, how dainty, how pointy, what fabulous color, what beautiful embroidery, what wonderful stitches. My shoes are fleeting moments. My biggest kick in life, if I only achieve one thing, is to entertain people."[3]

Trends in footwear have always been fueled by fashion at large, with designers often creating models to effectively underscore a particular silhouette in vogue. With the pluralistic character of contemporary fashion, from lean, hard-edged looks to frilly party dresses, we are witnessing revivals and reinterpretations of every major twentieth-century style. Flat-heeled styles continue to grow in importance, especially during the day. But designers whose clothes embody a more modern approach to dressing, such as Romeo Gigli, are showing elegant flats for

L inen and suede day pump by Manolo
BLAHNIK, 1991. (Manolo Blahnik,
London.) [151]

Above, *satin couture shoes by Christian LACROIX, summer 1988. (Christian Lacroix, Paris.)* [152]

Collage *by Roger VIVIER, cut paper, 1991. (Roger Vivier, Paris.)* [153]

evening as well, a concept pioneered by Vionnet, Chanel, and others from earlier in the century. The idea makes sense today when it's not uncommon for very social women to attend several events in the course of an evening. But the fashion magazines haven't followed suit. Whenever the couture collections are presented, the models are almost always shown wearing rapturously high-heeled evening shoes. Some manufacturers are attempting to marry the comfort and cushioning of athletic shoes—the area in which the true

technical advances in footwear are being made today—with daytime styles suitable for working women. The concept is brilliant, but to date the execution has not been as stylistically refined as it could be.

With the "anything goes" nature of contemporary fashion and footwear, one might expect that perhaps shoes no longer indicate much about women's social position, as they have over the centuries. But indeed they still seem to. For instance, more and more executive women—those who have won

E mbroidered leather pumps by MODEL, 1984, fabricated by René Caovilla of Venice, one of the last artisan workshops for fine hand-embroidery of shoes. (Philippe Model, Paris.)   [155]

"S irène," by Philippe MODEL, 1985–86—mermaid shoe in suede and snakeskin. (Philippe Model, Paris.)   [154]

"Egg" prototype by LOUBOUTIN in satin with natural wood heel, 1988. (Christian Louboutin, Paris.) [156]

Striped satin evening pumps by Emma HOPE, 1991. [157]

acceptance at the top level in the workplace—have begun to wear high heels at the office instead of practical low-heeled pumps. Professional women used to wear only sensible shoes to proclaim their seriousness, but today, high heels have become a symbol of clout. "Apparently the flat-sole influence of the '60s and '70s is fading," observed writer Francine Prose, "and the extremely high heel (along with that other great comfort item, the mini-skirt) is currently moving back into the boardroom, the editorial office, the TV studio—the footholds of politics, power, and visibility that women have only recently and marginally achieved."[4] Certainly there are a great many women at all levels who commute in sneakers and put on their heels at the office, and others who have become used to wearing them all day. But Prose has suggested that at least some executive women are wearing high heels to set themselves apart from women below their level—a subtle sign that they can afford to taxi to work rather than deal with public transportation. Remembering the Venetian noblewomen of the Renaissance who distinguished themselves by wearing platforms so high that they needed a servant to accompany them, this aspect

of women's footwear seems to have changed very little over the past five hundred years.

The trend toward high heels in the workplace in some ways looks like a cruel fashion joke whose punch line combines discomfort and exploitation. But for women at the top who are no longer fearful of not being taken seriously, wearing high heels can be a sign of self-assurance. And a few more inches of height can be a decided asset in the workplace, a world that is still very much a male domain in which height is equated with power. No matter how impractical, frivolous, dangerous, or outdated, high heels will always be with us. Like smoking or wearing fur, they remain an element of fashion or lifestyle that to some women will always stand for glamour and elegance.

The most inventive, ornate, and superbly-crafted shoes created in recent years are the prototypes that Roger Vivier created for a stunning exhibition devoted to his work at Paris's Musée des Arts de la Mode in winter of 1987–88. Of the four hundred models shown, more than half were new creations. Some were masterfully simple, but in other opulently beaded models Vivier displayed the classic fantasy and finesse that made his shoes

"Ouambam," cuissarde boots by LOUBOUTIN, 1984, in palm bark with laces and lining in natural leather. (Christian Louboutin, Paris.) [158]

Left, satin evening boots by VIVIER, 1987, embroidered with satin flowers; created for an exhibition of Vivier's work in Paris. (Musée des Arts de la Mode, Paris. Collection of Union Française des Arts du Décoratifs.) [159]

Right, VIVIER, surrounded by the shoes he exhibited in Paris, 1987.   [160]

"Goya" by VIVIER, 1987, with comma heel. Fabricated by René Caovilla of Venice, the shoes were made by cutting patent leather into a mosaic pattern, wrapping it with silk thread, and backing it with leather strips—a process requiring thirty hours of handwork for each pair." (Private collection, New York.)   [161]

for Dior in the 1950s some of the most extraordinary ever created. Working with the house of Lesage, which fabricates the embroidery for most of the couture houses in Paris, Vivier created a magnificent group of high *cuissarde* evening boots in velvet and satin—a level of haute couture unsurpassed in the realm of contemporary footwear. Although these shoes were designed solely for exhibition, Vivier created them with the level of quality, craft, and invention that has always characterized his work, and then donated the entire collection to the museum. It is a sad comment on the commercial possibilities of elaborate craftsmanship that these magnificent creations were never produced for sale—a telling sign that the couture industry today makes its profits from perfume and licensing and not from creating pieces of *grand luxe*.

The métier of designing shoes has been described as a sculptural process, yet considering that the form of the shoe must also serve a function, it might also be viewed as an architectural endeavor. Shoe trends come and go, representing points on the pendulum that swings back and forth between comfort and style—between the functional and the abstract or purely visual. Witnessing the success some designers have had recently in offering narrow lasts and long, pointed toes, it is evident that an attractive silhouette continues to be an important factor for many women when it comes to choosing footwear. Shoes in our century have run the gamut from stylishly comfortable to magnificently impractical—a vast and varied repertoire from which a woman can choose the shoes that allow her to put her best foot forward.

NOTES

Introduction

1. Eugenia Girotti, *La Calzatura, Storia e costume* (Milan: BE-MA Editrice, 1986), p. 134.

2. Charles Higham, *The Duchess of Windsor: The Secret Life* (New York: McGraw-Hill, 1988), p. 87.

3. Johann Wolfgang von Goethe, *Letters from Goethe*, translated by M. von Herzfeld and C. Melvil Sym (Edinburgh: University Press, 1957), p. 320.

4. Simon Braun, "La douleur, le pied et la chaussure," in *Revue de l'Institut de Calcéologie* 3, p. 23.

5. Ibid. p. 23.

6. J. J. Matignon, *Superstition: Crime et misère en Chine* (Paris: Masson, 1899), p. 220.

7. June Swann, interview with the author, Northampton, England, November 1988.

8. Aimee Liu and Meg Rottman, *Shoe Time* (New York: Arbor House, 1986), p. 1.

9. Swann.

Chapter One

1. Marcel Proust, *Remembrance of Things Past*, translated by C.K. Scott Moncrieff and Frederick A. Blossom (New York: Random House, 1927–32), p. 1162.

2. William Edward Winks, *Lives of Illustrious Shoemakers* (New York: Funk & Wagnalls, 1883), p. iv.

3. Edmonde Charles-Roux, *Chanel and Her World* (New York: Vendome Press, 1979), p. 59.

4. Cornelia Otis Skinner, *Elegant Wits and Grand Horizontals* (Boston: Houghton Mifflin, 1962), p. 231.

5. Charles-Roux, p. 120.

6. Diana Vreeland, *American Women of Style* (New York: The Metropolitan Museum of Art, 1975).

7. Cecil Beaton, *The Glass of Fashion* (Garden City, N.Y.: Doubleday, 1954), p. 147.

8. Mercedes De Acosta, *Here Lies the Heart* (New York: Reynal, 1960), p. 47.

9. Beaton, p. 147.

10. De Acosta, p. 48.

11. June Swann, *Shoes* (London: B.T. Batsford, 1982), p. 51.

12. *La Voce d'Italia*, February 22, 1949.

13. Brigid Keenan, *The Women We Wanted to Look Like* (London: Macmillan, 1977), p. 11.

14. Stephania Ricci, "From Artisan to Couturier," in *Salvatore Ferragamo: Art of the Shoe* (Florence: Centro Di, 1987), p. 27

15. Ibid.

Chapter Two

1. Carolyn Hall, *The Forties in Vogue*, (New York: Harmony Books, 1985), p. 62.

2. Diana Vreeland, *D.V.* (New York: Random House, 1985), p. 125.

3. Brochure from Brouwer's Research Lasts, in William Rossi, *The Sex Life of the Foot and Shoe* (New York: Saturday Review Press, 1976), p. 156.

4. June Swann, *Shoes* (London: B.T. Batsford, 1982), p. 58.

5. Brigid Keenan, *The Women We Wanted to Look Like* (London: Macmillan, 1977), p. 16.

6. Roger Vivier, interview with the author, Paris, December 1987.

7. *Hamlet*, act II, scene II, lines 136–37.

8. *Documenta-Moda* (summer 1942), cited in *Salvatore Ferragamo: Art of the Shoe* (Florence: Centro Di, 1987), p. 141.

9. Hall, p. 8.

10. Vreeland, p. 150.

11. Hall, p. 62.

12. Eleanor Lambert, *The World of Fashion* (New York: Bowker, 1976), p. 333.

13. Nancy Jaslow, "During World War II Footwear Was Put on Rations," *Footwear News*, October 6, 1985, p. 20.

14. Hall, p. 20.

Chapter Three

1. William Rossi, *The Sex Life of the Foot and Shoe* (New York: Saturday Review Press, 1976), p. 123.

2. Ibid., p. 225.

3. June Swann, *Shoes* (London: B.T. Batsford, 1982), p. 81.

4. *Les Souliers de Roger Vivier* (Paris: Musée des Arts de la Mode, 1987), p. 52.

5. A. Jacoby, "Shoe Manufacturers Are Villains," *Footwear* (England) July 1959, p. 40.

6. David Kunzle, *Fashion and Fetishism: A Social History of Corsets, Tight-lacing and Other Forms of Body Sculpting in the West* (Totowa, N.J.: Rowman & Littlefield), p. 183.

7. Jacoby, p. 38.

8. Rossi, p. 123.

9. Ibid., p. 124.

10. Carolyn Hall, *The Forties in Vogue* (New York: Harmony Books, 1985), p. 20.

11. Simone de Beauvoir, quoted in Hall, p. 17.

12. Rossi, p. 30.

13. "Le Fetichisme de la chaussure," *Union* 101 (November 1980), p. 13.

14. M. Lauret, president of club 50/60, quoted in *Elle*, June 25, 1984.

15. Vivian Infantino, "Shoe Fashions 1945–85," *Footwear News*, October 6, 1985, p. 16.

16. Pierre Provoyeur, "Des Souliers de Collection," in *Les Souliers de Roger Vivier* (Paris: Musée des Arts de la Mode, 1987), p. 16.

17. Vivier, interview with the author, Paris, December 1987.

18. Diana Vreeland, *D.V.* (New York: Random House, 1985), p. 213.

19. Michel Brodsky, interview with the author, Paris, December 1987.

20. Valerie Seckler, "When American Shoe Lions Roared," *Footwear News*, October 6, 1985, p. 2

21. Charline Osgood, presentation boards and papers, archives of Brooklyn Museum, Brooklyn, New York.

22. Salvatore Ferragamo, *Shoemaker of Dreams* (London: Harrap & Co., 1957), p. 219.

Chapter Four

1. Nancy Sinatra, from her hit record, "These Boots Are Made for Walkin'," 1966, by Lee Hazelwood.

2. *Footwear News*, October 6, 1985, p. 15.

3. Diana Vreeland, telephone interview with the author, 1987.

4. Yves Saint Laurent, in *Roger Vivier* (Bordeaux: Centre Sigma Lainé, 1980), p. 194.

5. Diana Vreeland, telephone interview with the author, 1987.

6. Michel Brodsky, interview with the author, Paris, December 1987.

7. Diana Vreeland. *D.V.* (New York: Random House, 1985), p. 194.

Chapter Five

1. Thomas Carlyle, in Robert Andrews, ed., *The Routledge Dictionary of Quotations* (London: Routledge and Kegan, 1987), p. 56.

BIBLIOGRAPHY

Baynes, Kate, and Ken Baynes. *The Shoe Show: British Shoes since 1790*. London: Crafts Council, 1979.

Bertin, Celia. *Paris à la Mode*. London: Collanca, 1956.

The Boot and Shoe Industry in Northampton. Northampton England: Northamptonshire Libraries, 1976.

Brooke, Iris. *Footwear: A Short History of European and American Shoes*. New York: Theatre Arts Books, 1971.

Ferragamo, Salvatore. *Shoemaker of Dreams*. London: Harrap & Co., 1957.

Girotti, Eugenia. *La Calzatura, Storia e Costume*. Milan: BE-MA Editrice, 1986.

Klaw, Irving. *Cartoon and Model Parade*. New York: Klaw, 1950.

Lambert, Eleanor. *The World of Fashion*. New York: Bowker, 1976.

Levy, Howard. *Chinese Foot Binding*. New York: Bell Publishing, 1972.

Liu, Aimee, and Meg Rottman. *Shoe Time*. New York: Arbor House, 1986.

McDowell, Colin. *McDowell's Directory of 20th Century Fashion*. Englewood Cliffs, N.J.: Prentice-Hall, 1985.

Pond, Mimi. *Shoes Never Lie*. New York: Berkley Publishing, 1985.

Probert, Christina. *Shoes in Vogue since 1910*. New York: Abbeville, 1981.

Revue de L'Institut de Calcéologie 1–3 (1982–86).

Roger Vivier. Bordeaux, France: Centre Sigma Lainé, 1980.

Rossi, William. *The Sex Life of the Foot and Shoe*. New York: Saturday Review Press, 1976.

Roux, Jean-Paul. *La Chaussure*. Paris: Hachette, 1980.

Salvatore Ferragamo: Art of the Shoe. Florence: Centro Di, 1987.

Les Souliers de Roger Vivier. Paris: Musée des Arts de la Mode, 1987.

Steele, Valerie. *Paris Fashion: A Cultural History*. New York: Oxford University, 1988.

Sulser, Wilhelm. *A Brief History of the Shoe*. Schoenenwerd, Switzerland: Bally Shoe Museum, 1958 (reprint).

Swann, June. *A History of Shoe Fashions*. Northampton, England: Northampton Borough Council, 1975.

———. *Shoes*. London: B.T. Batsford, 1985.

Villeneuve, Roland. *Fetichisme et amour*. Paris: Editions Azur, 1982.

Vreeland, Diana. *D.V.* New York: Random House, 1985.

Wilcox, R. T. *The Mode in Footwear*. New York: Scribners, 1948.

Wilson, Elizabeth. *Adorned in Dreams: Fashion and Modernity*. London: Virago, 1985.

Wilson, Eunice. *A History of Shoe Fashions*. London: Putnam, 1969.

Winks, William. *Lives of Illustrious Shoemakers*. New York: Funk & Wagnalls, 1883.

INDEX

Photography Credits